Prince 2 Workbook

TABLE OF CONTENTS

INTRODUCING PRINCE 2

Project Management and introducing Prince2

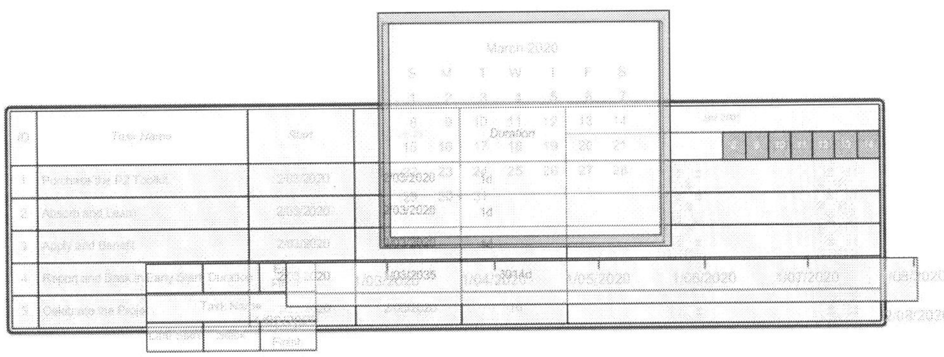

Prince2 Community Forum: www.p2ug.com

PRINCE® is a registered trade mark of OGC (www.ogc.gov.uk)

Let's agree that a project...

- Is a relatively short term endeavour with the purpose to create a unique product or service
- Has to deliver measurable beneifts to the organization that is undertaking the project
- Needs to be managed in some form to maximize the chances of success

Prince2 Community Forum: www.p2ug.com

The most important part...Business Benefits

- Direct Benefits
  - Cost controls
  - Increased Revenue
- Indirect benefits
  - Greater Control
  - Higher Market Share
  - Higher Quality
  - Potential to lower head count
  - Standardized method for new product introduction

Prince2 Community Forum: www.p2ug.com

PRINCE® is a registered trade mark of OGC (www.ogc.gov.uk)

The great news with direct benefits is that they are MEASURABLE. Emphasize this point, as business people want to see tangible results – they want the intangibles of indirect benefits as well, but given the choice they will take cost saving and increased revenues.

Today's projects are often...

- New, groundbreaking, never been done
- Laced with vague, unclear and ambiguous objectives
- Poorly defined Requirements that have no flexibility for change, as circumstances change
- Unclear steps and no boundaries
  - Poor Time and Cost Management
  - A "somehow" approach to delivery of benefits

Prince2 Community Forum: www.p2ug.com

This page aims to raise the awareness of what the major areas of weakness are for poorly managed projects.

It is for these reasons that we need a structure, REPEATABLE method that all parties can learn.

So the challenge for today's project

- Transform poorly defined requirements into actual measurable deliverables
  - "improved performance" ✗
  - "23% improvement to be realized within 12 business days" ✓
- Having the best customer satisfaction rating is irrelevant if sales of ZERO
  - Business runs on results, numbers, facts and figures
  - Projects designed to deliver business benefits must be measured, as must the benefits they intend to deliver.
- Adopt flexible practices.
  - Everything changes.
  - It's a fact, so don't be surprised when it happens

The supervisor says at the start of the week; "This week I want you to make 20 calls to clients". At the end of the week the sales person reports in. The supervisor asks; "How many calls did you make?".

The news sales person replies; "Well........"... ALARM BELLS start to ring... "well...." is not a number – you can't measure "Well..."

But the new sales person says; "but you don't understand, let me tell you the WHOLE STORY about what went wrong"...
The supervisor needs to reply' "... I don't have room in this little box for an entire story, it's only designed to hold a number AND the NUMBER TELLS ME THE WHOLE STORY"

Please see Project Support Role Definition on page 67 within this workbook.

Prince2

- PRINCE2, Projects IN Controlled Environments
- Project management method covering the organization, management and control of projects.
- Process Based & Product Based
- Project Board integral component for authorisation
- Project Stages and Gates
- Defines responsibility, authority and accountability reducing confusion
- Divides the project into manageable stages for more accurate planning

Prince2 Community Forum: www.p2ug.com

PRINCE® is a registered trade mark of OGC (www.ogc.gov.uk)

PRINCE2 offers a process-based approach for project management. It provides a tailored and scalable method for the management of all types of projects. Each process is defined with its key inputs and outputs together with the specific objectives and activities to be performed. Prince2 describes the projects manageable stages – which allows efficient control of resources and regular progress monitoring throughout the project.

Project planning using PRINCE2 is product-based. This means project plans are aimed at delivering results (not just about planning when the various activities on the project will take place).

Integral to PRINCE2 method is the business case. The business case describes the organization's justification, commitment and rationale for the project's itself. The business case has to be reviewed on a regular basis to ensure the business objectives are still being met (especially important when these objectives can change over time).

Prince2

- PRINCE2, Projects IN Controlled Environments
- Project management method covering the organization, management and control of projects.
- Process Based & Product Based
- Project Board integral component for authorisation
- Project Stages and Gates
- Defines responsibility, authority and accountability reducing confusion
- Divides the project into manageable stages for more accurate planning

Prince2 Community Forum www.p2ug.com

Continued…

The method (like the ITIL Framework for IT process management of infrastructure environments) provides a common language across all parties (including external third parties).

PRINCE2 can be used for a wide variety of projects.

INTRODUCING PRINCE 2 EXTENDED

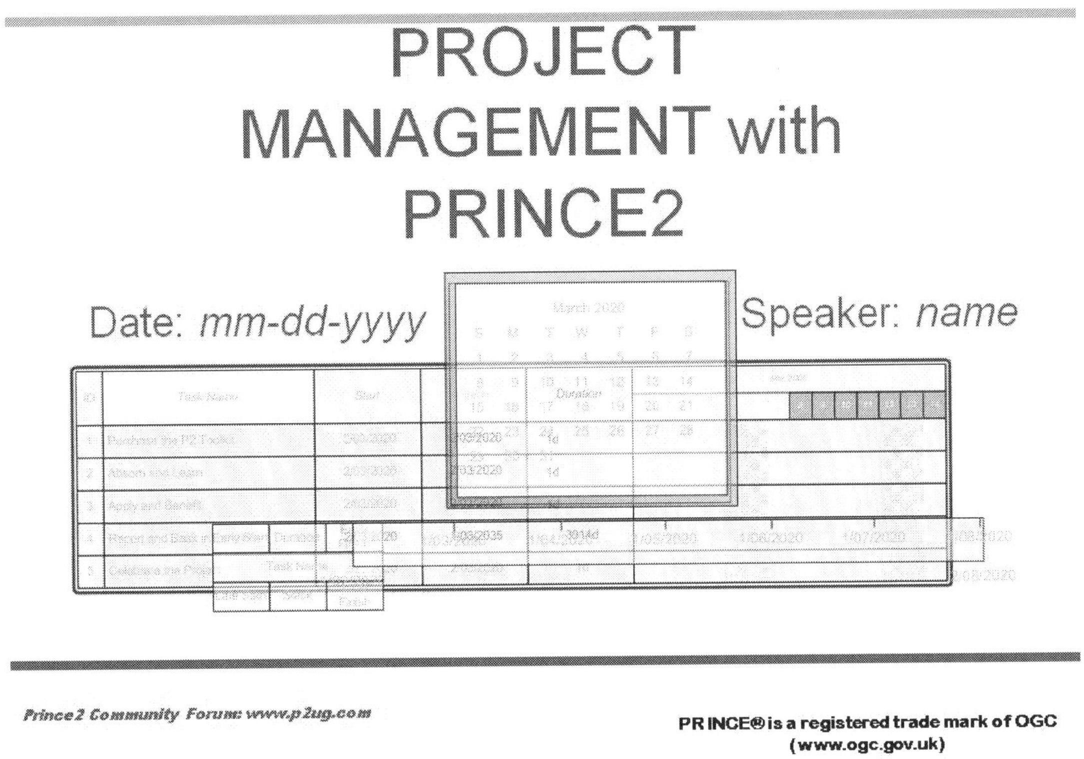

This longer PowerPoint show gives you an introduction into the Prince2 framework. Still an introduction, but the focus is specifically on the Prince2 method itself and in particular the Prince2 processes are presented.

Prince2 - Agenda

- Prince2 Basics
- The Business Case
- Prince2 Components
- Prince2 Processes
- Summary and Questions

Prince2 Community Forum: www.p2ug.com

PRINCE® is a registered trade mark of OGC (www.ogc.gov.uk)

Please refer to the Prince 2 Fact Sheet Document on page 69 within this workbook

Introduction to PRINCE2

Introduction

- Projects in Controlled Environments
- A project management methodology adopted by British Government for all IT projects
- Created in the early 1990's
- Widely used in public and private sectors and has become UK's de facto standard for project management

Prince2 Community Forum: www.p2ug.com

Please refer to Project Manager Role Description on page 71 within this workbook.

PRINCE2
The Business Case

- Prince2 projects characterized by the "business case"
- Describes the justification and the expected outcome for the project
- Business case must be regularly reviewed as part of Project

Prince2 Community Forum: www.p2ug.com

PRINCE® is a registered trade mark of OGC (www.ogc.gov.uk)

The Business case is paramount with regard to Prince2.

Failure to deliver products that provide the benefits mapped out in the business case equates to a failed project.

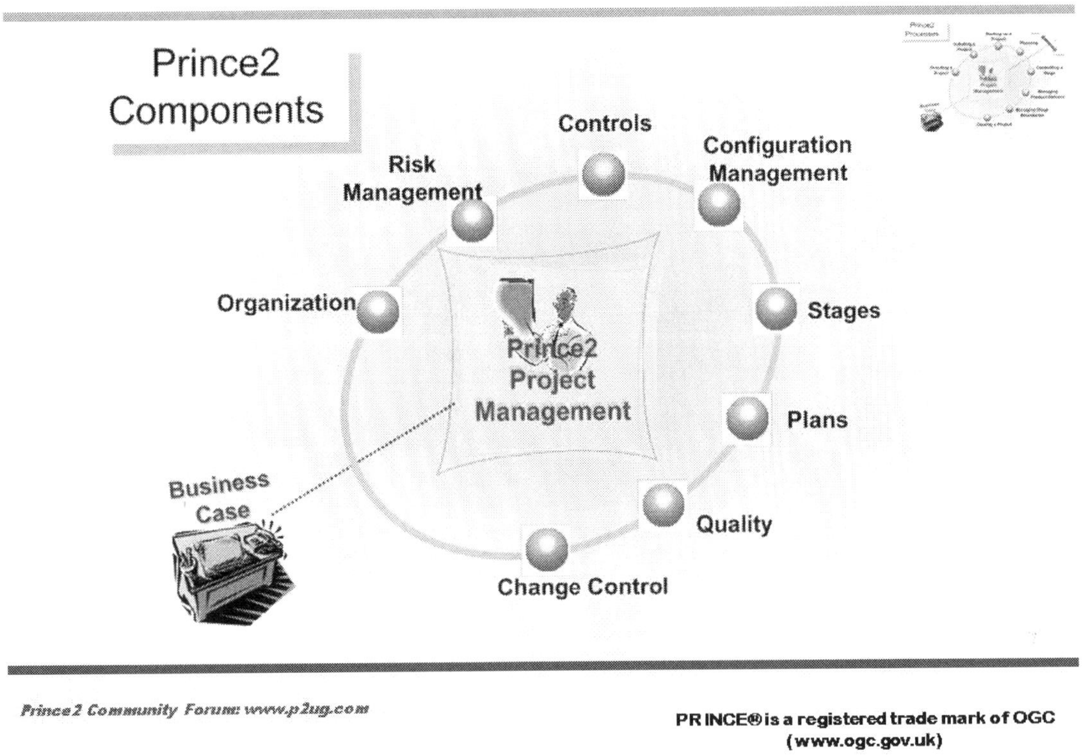

Now we will look at the 8 component considerations that influence and support the Prince2 processes (which are covered later).

PRINCE2 Components

❖ Organization

- 'Supplier' and 'Customer' concept
- **Project** Management Team
  - ❑ Four layer principle
- **Program** Organization

Prince2 Community Forum: www.p2ug.com

It is almost superfluous to say that an effective organizational structure for the project is vital.
So we will assume that is known and look at the way the Prince2 defines the "organization" of a project.

'Supplier' and 'Customer' concept – simple premise that the customer is the party that pays for the project. Note the supplier need not be an "external to the organization" party.

Project Management Team
Project Board – represents (at management level) the business
Executive – ultimate accountability for the project, focus on return on investment.

PRINCE2 Components

❖ Organization

- 'Supplier' and 'Customer' concept
- **Project** Management Team
  - ❑ Four layer principle
- **Program** Organization

Continued…

Senior User – represents the users and makes sure that the products to be delivered are clearly defined and fit for purpose when they are delivered.
Senior Supplier – has a focus on delivering the requirements of the Senior User (within typical constraints)

Project Manager – day-to-day management of the project
Team Leader – an optional role, where teams of specialists are used on specific products/activities then the Project Manager may require a Single Point of Contact

Project Assurance – the Project Board need an assurance that the project is going according to the reports they will receive from the Project Manager
Project Support – optional, administrative support for the Project Manager

Four layer principle – Prince2 claims that a project organization has 4 layers of activity.
Direction of the project (Project Management Team)
Day-to-day project management (Project Management Team)
Team Management (Project Management Team)
The actual work to create products (Team members)

PRINCE2 Components

❖ Organization

- 'Supplier' and 'Customer' concept
- **Project** Management Team
  - ❑ Four layer principle
- **Program** Organization

Prince2 Community Forum: www.p2ug.com

Continued…

Program Organization - (when a project is one of many projects).
Program Director – overall responsibility for all projects. Will delegate authority for projects to a Project Board.
Change Manager – Projects result in change to the way the organization operates. The Change Manager role is to author and guard the business case that results in a project. They become the coordinating force between the project deliverables and the implementation of the deliverables into the organization.
Design Authority – the project management policy, it's procedures, it's information flows must be design and improved. The Design Authority looks at policies to ensure compliance and will proactively look for improvements. They are responsible for ensuring that all projects follow the accepted path.
Program Manager – The day to day management of the overall Program. They represent the Program Director and work closely with the Project Managers (to support them and ensure information is flowing). The Program Manager is also responds to project exceptions, slippages and changes in priority. It is a linking role between the Program organization and the projects themselves.

Please see Project Manager Role Description on page 73 within this workbook.

PRINCE2 Components

❖ Management of Risk

- Types of risk
  - Business Risk
  - Project Risk
- Risk Management
  - Analysis
  - Management

Prince2 Community Forum: www.p2ug.com

PRINCE® is a registered trade mark of OGC (www.ogc.gov.uk)

You can mention here that Risk Management is an entire area of study in its own right.

For example the OGC has a Risk Management methodology called. CRAMM (CCTA Risk Analysis and Management Methodology) (CCTA was the original name of the OGC – Office of Government Commerce)

PRINCE2 defines risk as:

'The chance of exposure to the adverse consequences of future events.'

Key role of Project Manager is the overall management of risk

Types of risk

Business Risk – "things" outside the project that threaten the ability of the project to deliver the products that will lead to the expected business benefits (e.g. validity of the business case, legislative changes, environmental issues, change in strategic direction)

PRINCE2 Components

❖ Management of Risk

- Types of risk
  - ❑ Business Risk
  - ❑ Project Risk
- Risk Management
  - ❑ Analysis
  - ❑ Management

Prince2 Community Forum: www.p2ug.com

PRINCE® is a registered trade mark of OGC (www.ogc.gov.uk)

Continued…

Project Risk – "things" inside the project that threaten the ability of the project to deliver the products that will lead to the expected business benefits (e.g. issues with suppliers, skills shortage, lack of project management expertise, personality clashes).

Risk Management

Project Board advises Project Manager of Business Risks, Project Manager advises Project Board of Project risks.

Analysis – the identification, estimation (impact) and evaluation (likelihood)

5 strategies – Prevention, Reduction, Transference (assign the risk to a third party e.g. insurance)), Contingency (action to take if the risk eventuates), Acceptance

Management

PLANNING – what will be done if a risk eventuates

RESOURCING – reflected in Stage Plans – who will do what should a risk eventuate

MONITORING – measures to ensure that if risks eventuate they can be recognized and invoke some action

CONTROLLING – making sure that the pre-defined plan for a risk manifestation are followed

PRINCE2 Components

❖ Controls

- ➢ Controlled Start
- ➢ Controlled Progress
- ➢ Controlled Close

- ➢ Major Control points
  - ❑ Project Initiation and Project Close
  - ❑ End Stage Assessment
  - ❑ Mid-Stage Assessment
  - ❑ Highlight Reports
  - ❑ Exception Reports

Prince2 Community Forum: www.p2ug.com

Core to the study of Project Management is the requirement to make decisions.

Quite simply, 'controls' allow decisions to be made.

In a project sense controls ensure that progress is producing the required products, according to schedule and cost constraints AND that the business case viability is still valid.

Controlled Start – links in with the Starting up a Project (SP) and Initiating a Project (IP) processes (see later)

Controlled Progress – ties in with reviews of progress against current stage plans and reflection of the Project Initiation Document (PID)

Controlled Close – to ensure proper handover to support and that reviews are completed so lessons can be learned.

Major Control points

- Project Initiation and Project Close
- End Stage Assessment
- Mid-Stage Assessment
- Highlight Reports
- Exception Reports
-

PRINCE2 Components

❖Configuration Management

➢Consists of five basic functions:
- ❑ planning
- ❑ identification
- ❑ control
- ❑ status accounting
- ❑ verification

Prince2 Community Forum: www.p2ug.com

PRINCE® is a registered trade mark of OGC (www.ogc.gov.uk)

Central to effective Project Management is the delivery of products that will be used to realize benefits for the business.

Configuration Management identifies, tracks and protects these products. Even more important in a Program, as inter project product transfers could take place.

The five basic functions of Configuration Management are repeated as the activities for the Configuration Management process under ITIL (IT Infrastructure Library) – an IT infrastructure process improvement framework – also owned by the OGC

Configuration Management is **not optional** – the only flexibility is the degree of formality with which it is undertaken.
Planning – what level will products be identified, who will identify, gather, update records, etc.

PRINCE2 Components

❖ Configuration Management

- Consists of five basic functions:
  - planning
  - identification
  - control
  - status accounting
  - verification

Prince2 Community Forum: www.p2ug.com

PRINCE® is a registered trade mark of OGC (www.ogc.gov.uk)

Continued…

Identification – actual product identification (can include actual labelling)
Control – how do we "freeze" product configurations, who can make changes to products if approved
Status accounting – tracking the development of a product
Verification – auditing that the products we think we have (based on records) actually exist in reality

PRINCE2 Components

❖ Stages

A collection of activities and products whose delivery is managed as single unit

- Management stages and Technical stages
- Time focussed
- Consecutive

We have to break the project into Stages.
The final number and size of each stage is dependent on the project.

Use of stages will provide us with:
Review and decision points – a set point for review/decision – not just an ad-hoc corridor conversation. Planning horizons – creates a shorter time focus. Project Plan covers the whole project and will need to be altered as circumstances alter. A stage plan is relatively short term focus and will therefore be less prone to modification.

Scalability – a project can be two to two hundred stages. The requirements of stage is the same throughout.
Management stages – e.g. resource allocation, reviews
Technical stages – based on product/s to be delivered as a result of the stage
Time focused - Generally projects are broken into stages based on the Project plan timeframe.
Consecutive - It is general practice that one stage must end, before the next stage can start.

PRINCE2 Components

❖ Plans

- ➢ Plan makeup
- ➢ Levels of Planning
- ➢ Approvals

Prince2 Community Forum: www.p2ug.com

PRINCE® is a registered trade mark of OGC (www.ogc.gov.uk)

Planning is not trivial, but it delivers a host of benefits.
Chiefly planning gives us ways to approach the achievement of business requirements (customer requirements).

Plan Makeup
The plan must specify what is to be achieved (products to be produced), activities required to deliver the products, required resources, time scales involved, activity dependence, potential risks, control and measurement points.

Levels
If appropriate the PROGRAM plan will be the input for each Project Plan
Project Plan – overview of the entire project and is part of the Project Initiation Document (PID)
Stage Plan – derived from the Project Plan a more detailed, but shorter time frame plan to achieve specific deliverables

PRINCE2 Components

❖ Plans

- Plan makeup
- Levels of Planning
- Approvals

Prince 2 Community Forum: www.p2ug.com

Continued…

Team Plan – OPTIONAL – take the stage plan and break it down for specialist members or teams.
Exception Plan (can be applied to Project, Stage or Team) – when tolerances are exceeded and it should include the reason why the plan is required – if required the exception plan typically replaces a Stage Plan.

Approvals

Consideration regarding who will approve various plans is important. This will be pre-defined, but a degree of common sense can also be applied here. (e.g. Project Plan and perhaps Stage Plans approved by the Project Board). Team Plans approved by the Project Manager.

Please refer to Plan and Project Document on page 75 within this workbook.

PRINCE2 Components

❖ Quality in a Project Environment

- Product descriptions
- Quality Reviews
- Link to ISO 9001

Prince2 Community Forum: www.p2ug.com

PRINCE® is a registered trade mark of OGC (www.ogc.gov.uk)

Quality is the concept that we use to discuss the suitability of a product for the purpose that is was designed or developed for. In a project environment we use quality to assess the suitability of products – but in regard to the context of the WHOLE project – not just the part of the project that the product was created under.

Quality Management will have four areas of focus if we are to ensure that the expectations of the customer are met.

- Quality System: Customer and supplier may have quality systems, that Prince2 and other frameworks (e.g. Cobit, ITIL) can be part of.
- Quality Assurance: Establishing a quality system is an initiation step. To ensure actual quality and that the system is followed, we need to design an ongoing activity for monitoring, reporting, reviewing, improving.

PRINCE2 Components

❖ Quality in a Project Environment

- Product descriptions
- Quality Reviews
- Link to ISO 9001

Continued…

- Quality Planning: Integrated into the Starting up a Project (SU) process; the way that the quality system will be used will be in the Project Initiation Document and therefore it will form part of each Stage Plan.
- Quality Control: Checking the quality of products produced matches the quality expectations and was reached by utilizing the Quality system.
- Product descriptions – quality reviews may result in a need to redefine products. If such a change is required, then Change Control must be involved.
- Quality Reviews – must be carried out at pre-determined intervals
- Link to ISO 9001 – ISO 9001 compliance is essentially that an organization will have a quality system in place. The overall organization Quality Management System, should include an element regarding the Quality of projects. This will then be reflected in the Project Quality Plan (which is typically integrated into the overall Project Plan).

PRINCE2 Components

❖ Change Control

- Post acceptance change
- Authority Levels
- Integrity of Change (interdependence)

Prince2 Community Forum: www.p2ug.com

PRINCE® is a registered trade mark of OGC (www.ogc.gov.uk)

Everything changes. Yes, even your well controlled and expertly planned Project products and their requirements.

The discussion on Change Control centres on any changes to PRODUCTS (i.e. the primary deliverable component of a stage).

Post acceptance change – changes to completed products that have been accepted by the Project Board, CANNOT be changed unless approved by the Project Board.

Authority Levels – Who can authorize changes to products? How will changes be paid for? What role does the Program Management play in the change? Change responsibilities should be included in relevant job descriptions.

PRINCE2 Components

❖Change Control

- Post acceptance change
- Authority Levels
- Integrity of Change (interdependence)

Continued…

Integrity of Change – A change to one product can have flow on effects. Changes can be triggered from reviews of the Business case justification, from Risk Management activities, from organizational issues (strategic reviews, cost saving requirements, etc.)

In PRINCE, all project changes are managed as a formal Project Issue
Control of change means assessment of:
Impact of potential change importance cost. Approved changes must be reflected in project documentation

Please see Change Manager Role Description on page 91 within this workbook.

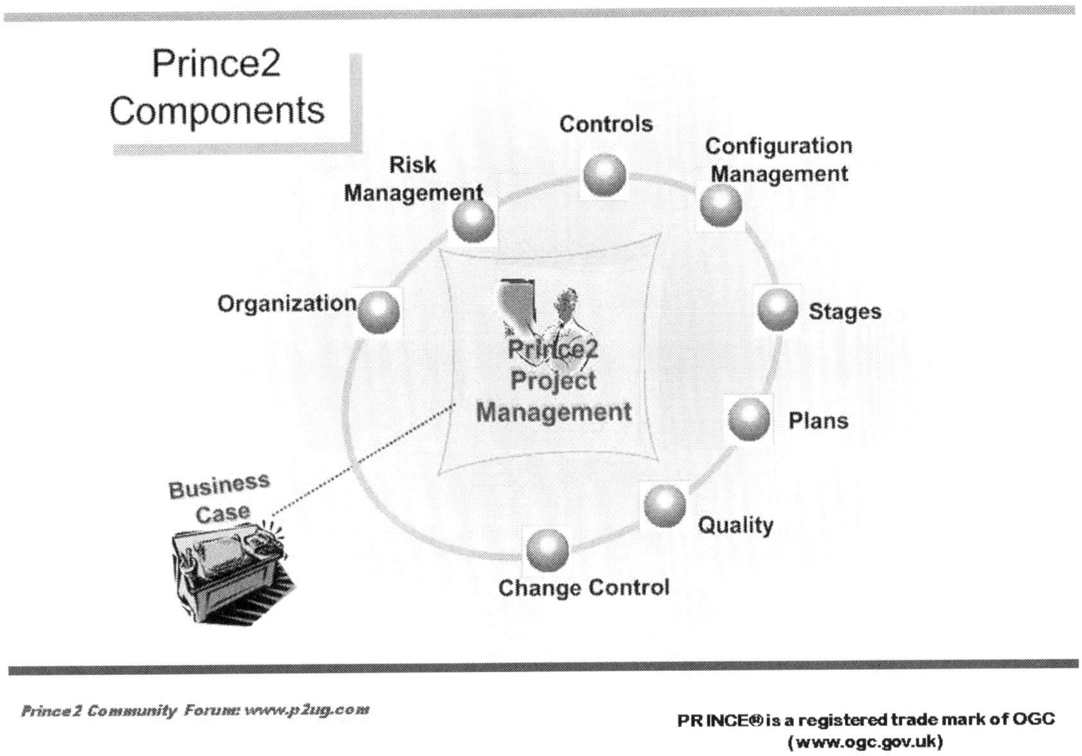
Prince2
Components
Controls
Configuration
Management
Risk
Management
Organization
Stages
Prince2
Project
Management
Plans
Business
Case
Quality
Change Control
Prince2 Community Forum: www.p2ug.com
PRINCE® is a registered trade mark of OGC
(www.ogc.gov.uk)

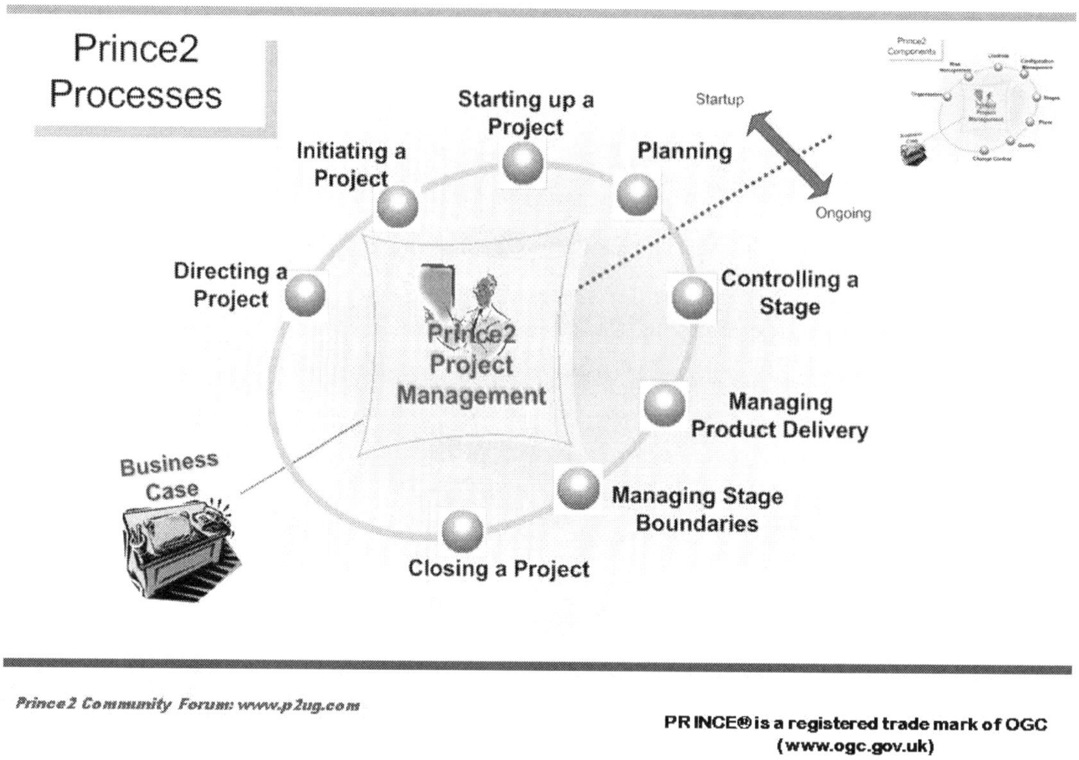

Now we will look at the 8 defined processes that comprise the Prince2 Framework.

You can see in this image that some processes have been labeled as "startup", others as "ongoing".

The "Directing a Project" is ongoing, but it is also more strategic in nature.

PRINCE2 Processes (SU)

❖Process STARTING UP A PROJECT

➢Pre-project activities

- ❑ Establish the Risk Log
- ❑ Project Brief
- ❑ Project Approach
- ❑ Initiation Stage Plan
- ❑ Appoint the Project Management Team

Prince2 Community Forum: www.p2ug.com

Logically the second process defined by Prince2 is SU = Starting up a Project (Note the first process (DP) is more and more of an CONTINUIM of activities that is required throughout the life of the project.)

This process can be thought of as the Pre-project activities and has the deliverables as named above.
Note: the next slide covers the roles for the Project Management Team (and the higher level Program Organization).

Project Brief – done to ensure that the project is actually VIABLE and will deliver benefits.
Project Approach – essentially how the project will be dealt with (e.g. purchase off the shelf, in house developed, outsourced)
Initiation Stage Plan – IF the project is to proceed, then the preparation or INITIATION of the project will take time, effort, resources. The Initiation Stage Plan outlines the expected time, effort, resources (and costs) of getting the project up and running.

PRINCE2

Project Management Team (1)

- The Project Board
  - Executive, Senior User, Senior Supplier
- Project Manager
- Team Leader
- Project Assurance
- Project Support

Prince2 Community Forum: www.p2ug.com

PRINCE® is a registered trade mark of OGC (www.ogc.gov.uk)

Part of the first process SU = Starting up a Project

Establishing the Project Management Team.. Note the distinction between this slide which deals with the PROJECT and the next slide which deals with the Program Management.

The role titles in this slide are related to a specific project.

Many projects in an organization, require program management to ensure that all projects share similar processes (helps to maximize the efficiency of all processes (reduce duplication and share lessons learned)

PRINCE2

Project Management Team (2)

- **Program Organization**
  - **Program Director**
  - **Change Manager**
  - **Design Authority**
  - **Program Manager**

Prince2 Community Forum: www.p2ug.com

PRINCE® is a registered trade mark of OGC (www.ogc.gov.uk)

Establishing the PROGRAM ORGANIZATION Team.. Note the distinction between this slide which deals with the PROGRAM Management and the previous slide which deals with the Project Management.

Many projects in an organization, require program management to ensure that all projects share similar processes (helps to maximize the efficiency of all processes (reduce duplication and share lessons learned).

Essentially these roles influence all projects.

Director – overall control, appoints Project Boards, secures resources, monitors progress, controls program management

Change Manager – responsible for all change activities and to ensure all parties are aware of changes and how benefits will flow from the changes

PRINCE2

Project Management Team (2)

- Program Organization
  - Program Director
  - Change Manager
  - Design Authority
  - Program Manager

Prince2 Community Forum: www.p2ug.com

PRINCE® is a registered trade mark of OGC (www.ogc.gov.uk)

Continued…

Design Authority – to ensure that any procedures, systems or parts of a specific project will "mesh" in with the overall Program (easiest example is for reporting).

Program Manager – Day-to-day operational management of the program (supports Project Managers), deals with exceptions, slips in timeframes and setting priorities. Is the link between the Program organization and the Projects.

PRINCE2 Processes (DP)

❖Process DIRECTING A PROJECT

➢Begins after Project Start Up (SU)

➢The Project Board will :

- ❑authorize project initiation
- ❑authorize the project
- ❑authorize a stage/exception plan
- ❑liaise with Program Management and
- ❑provide overall direction and management
- ❑confirm project closure

Prince2 Community Forum: www.p2ug.com

PRINCE® is a registered trade mark of OGC (www.ogc.gov.uk)

This process (DP) is more and more of an CONTINUIM of activities that is required throughout the life of the project. It begins AFTER the project START UP (SU) and runs through until the completion of the Project (refer CP – Closing a Project).

The Board is not involved with the day-to-day management of the project.

Note: the connection to the SU process. The board will base its decision to authorize the project initiation, based on the Initiation Stage Plan.

The actual project authorization comes from the Project Board. The decision is made in regard to the strength of the business case, balanced against the time, cost and other relevant organization strategies.

PRINCE2 Processes (DP)

❖Process DIRECTING A PROJECT

- Begins after Project Start Up (SU)
- The Project Board will :
  - authorize project initiation
  - authorize the project
  - authorize a stage/exception plan
  - liaise with Program Management and
  - provide overall direction and management
  - confirm project closure

Prince2 Community Forum: www.p2ug.com

Continued...

The project should be broken into manageable pieces. Each piece should be approved. This forces a review by the board and allows the board to ensure that the business case is still valid and make known to the project team any organizational changes that may influence the project.

The project closure is the formal handover of the project to the support or production environment of the organization.

PRINCE2 Processes (IP)

❖Process INITIATING A PROJECT

- ➢Planning Quality requirements
- ➢Planning the Project
- ➢Refining the Business Case & Risks
- ➢Establishing Project controls
- ➢Set up Project files
- ➢Create the Project Initiation Document (PID)

Prince2 Community Forum: www.p2ug.com

PRINCE® is a registered trade mark of OGC (www.ogc.gov.uk)

To date, the real work of the project has not begun. The activities prior to this point was to make sure that the project was not just a REACTION to a temporary issue.

Planning Quality requirements – review of the business case to ensure that WHAT is delivered matches the EXPECTATIONS of the customer

Planning the Project – this is establishing the control boundaries that will be used by the Project Board (timelines, events and costs).

Refining the Business Case & risks – all too often in the excitement of beginning a new project we lose sight of WHY the work is being done. This activity makes sure that we revisit the WHY question and look for ways that the outcome of the project will be missed (risks).

PRINCE2 Processes (IP)

❖Process INITIATING A PROJECT

- Planning Quality requirements
- Planning the Project
- Refining the Business Case & Risks
- Establishing Project controls
- Set up Project files
- Create the Project Initiation Document (PID)

Prince2 Community Forum: www.p2ug.com

PRINCE® is a registered trade mark of OGC (www.ogc.gov.uk)

Continued…

Establishing Project controls – the task of actually making decisions so that the project can proceed at the expected pace has to be established. This activity ensures that the proper communication, controls and monitoring are in place.

Set up Project files – a major challenge for any size project is the flow and control of information and documents. We need to have version control systems and ways to track information (note: the use of automated tools is crucial here and naturally this area is of specific interest to the PROGRAM MANAGEMENT organization.

Create the Project Initiation Document (PID) – This can be thought of as the SUMMARY of the entire project. Reading this document should answer to a degree the How, What, When, Who, When, Where, Why questions.

PRINCE2 Processes (PL)

- Process PLANNING
  - Designing a Plan
  - Product Definition + Analysis
  - Identify Activities and Dependencies
  - Estimating
  - Scheduling
  - Analysing Risks
  - Completing a Plan

Prince2 Community Forum: www.p2ug.com

PRINCE® is a registered trade mark of OGC (www.ogc.gov.uk)

Planning allows all involved parties to understand what is required, by who and when. The plan will describe certain events and resources required to deliver the requirements.

Designing a Plan – careful consideration must be given to what is to be included in the plan (Plan the plan !!)

Product Definition + Analysis – a crucial step is to be able to define WHAT is to be delivered. Not soft benefits, but measurable products.

Identify Activities and Dependencies – once we've defined the actual products for delivery, we need to identify the activities required to achieve it AND the relationships of activities to other product delivery activities (for workload balancing and to help avoid duplicated effort).

Estimating – clearly mark estimates as estimates. Using past experience and records. Learn from previous projects to help hone the estimating skill.

PRINCE2 Processes (PL)

- Process PLANNING
  - Designing a Plan
  - Product Definition + Analysis
  - Identify Activities and Dependencies
  - Estimating
  - Scheduling
  - Analysing Risks
  - Completing a Plan

Prince2 Community Forum: www.p2ug.com

PRINCE® is a registered trade mark of OGC (www.ogc.gov.uk)

Continued...

Scheduling – perhaps the "traditional view" of the Project plan. Now we look at all the activities that are required and put them into a system so we can see when each activity will be performed.

Analysing Risks – Risk analysis is an entire area of study. Suffice to say that improper consideration of risks will be the downfall of many – otherwise – valuable projects.

Completing a Plan – The plan is more than a GANTT or PERT chart, or a spreadsheet of figures. It is the drawing together of all of the plan information and presenting it in a clear and unambiguous manner.

Please refer to Risk Analysis Document on page 93 within this workbook.

PRINCE2 Processes (CS)

❖ Process CONTROLLING A STAGE

- Work Package authorization
- Assessing Progress
- Capturing Project issues
- Examining Project issues
- Reviewing Stage Status
- Reporting Highlights
- Taking Corrective Action
- Escalating Project Issues
- Receiving Completed Work Packages

Prince2 Community Forum: www.p2ug.com

Now that we have defined the "products" that are to be delivered, we need to ensure that we can actually deliver these products. Saying we can is one thing – actually doing it requires control disciplines. It requires discipline to ensure that resources don't get side tracked/distracted and it requires controls to ensure that the plan, along with its requisite budgets and time constraints are adhered to.

Work Package authorization – the trigger to begin a unit of work must come from the Project Manager
Assessing Progress – information flows about what is actually happening is compared to what was expected to happen
Capturing Project issues – things will go wrong and we must deal with these issues in a pre-defined and controlled manner
Examining Project issues – there are always many alternatives to dealing with a Project issue, we need to select the right (or "most right") one by studying the alternatives

PRINCE2 Processes (CS)

- Process CONTROLLING A STAGE
  - Work Package authorization
  - Assessing Progress
  - Capturing Project issues
  - Examining Project issues
  - Reviewing Stage Status
  - Reporting Highlights
  - Taking Corrective Action
  - Escalating Project Issues
  - Receiving Completed Work Packages

Continued…

Reviewing Stage Status – almost an enforced review to ensure that reviews are not treated as tiresome and mundane
Reporting Highlights – there is always good news to tell – the Project Board must be aware of the positives to ensure continued support and interest in the project.

Taking Corrective Action – there must be a process to follow for ALL corrective actions – even if they appear minor. Many small actions quickly add up to major problems – so ALL corrective action needs to be taken in a controlled fashion.
Escalating Project Issues – when a Project issue goes beyond the boundaries of what the Project manager can deal with (their tolerance limits), then the Project Board needs to be involved.. BUT as a Project Manager, bring the issue AND bring alternative solutions.
Receiving Completed Work Packages – Work packages that are DELIVERED (from the Managing Project Delivery Process) from individuals and/or teams are received back and then assessed to ensure that the work that was expected was actually done (and results (the status) reported to the Assessing Progress activity).

PRINCE2 Processes (MP)

❖Process MANAGING PRODUCT DELIVERY

- ➢ Accepting a Work Package
- ➢ Executing a Work Package
- ➢ Delivering a Work Package

Prince2 Community Forum: www.p2ug.com

Someone has to do the work !

We refer to the "someone" as third party Suppliers. We should also not get trapped in thinking that third party suppliers are only those external to the actual business. The Project generally calls upon internal staff to perform specific activities for the project – these staff then also become "third party suppliers".

Caution: beware of making this process a paper based nightmare of bureaucracy.

Accepting a Work Package – negotiation AND agreement with the third party supplier about what is to be asked of them and what constraints will apply (check for "reasonableness")

Executing a Work Package – remember the third parties may not be users of Prince2 or have any understanding of it. This should not affect their ability to perform the work that is asked of them. However, we do need to see that the work itself is managed and can be tracked/assessed.

PRINCE2 Processes (MP)

❖ Process MANAGING PRODUCT DELIVERY

- Accepting a Work Package
- Executing a Work Package
- Delivering a Work Package

Continued...

NB – Prince2 is not about directing people ***how*** to work, it is simply a way to ensure that the work that is done is matched to the required product delivery.

Delivering a Work Package – the end result of a work package is notification to the Project Manager that the work for that package has been completed.

PRINCE2 Processes (SB)

❖ Process MANAGING STAGE BOUNDARIES

- Planning a Stage
- Updating a Project Plan
- Updating a Project Business Case
- Updating the Risk Log
- Reporting Stage End
- Producing an Exception Plan

Prince2 Community Forum: www.p2ug.com

Perhaps the easiest way to think of this process is to consider the Guinness Book of World Records. Well, just one world record – for DOMINO toppling! Consider going for the world record in domino falling. As you build the record attempt you make breaks in the lines, so that if disaster strikes (someone knocks over a domino) the damage is limited to a relatively small area.

SB is building in the line breaks so that we can check the project is still on track to deliver the benefits. If it isn't then we can change direction or stop the project – without inflicting any more damage on the organization (principally cost).

Planning a Stage – a project is split into several stages. As one stage nears its end, we must be getting ready for the next stage – to ensure smooth continuity of product delivery. The next stage plan is derived from the overall Project Plan (prepared as part of the Planning (PL) process. The stage plan looks for Project Board support and ensures sufficient detail for day-to-day control purposes.

PRINCE2 Processes (SB)

❖Process MANAGING STAGE BOUNDARIES

- Planning a Stage
- Updating a Project Plan
- Updating a Project Business Case
- Updating the Risk Log
- Reporting Stage End
- Producing an Exception Plan

Prince2 Community Forum: www.p2ug.com

PRINCE® is a registered trade mark of OGC (www.ogc.gov.uk)

Continued…

Updating a Project Plan – We have discussed the changes of a project. As stages end and next stages begin, as issues arise and expectations are altered; all of this means that the Project Plan must be updated with new information.

Updating a Project Business Case – A critical consideration is to NOT lose sight of the fact that the Project is done to deliver benefits that will be explained in the business case. Therefore, as the business changes, so to will the business case for the project.

Updating the Risk Log – Keeping an up to date Risk log means that we are looking for potential and real ways that the project could be damaged. A single review of risks at the start of the project is simply not enough. It is a continual requirement.

Reporting Stage End – The people who approved the stage need to know when it's finished. The Project Board (and Program Management if applicable). Also any key stakeholders should be made aware of a stage end (E.g. Team Manager of third party suppliers).

Producing an Exception Plan – Exception is a departure or deviation beyond tolerance ranges. That is, minor deviations can be dealt with by the Project Manager directly (cross refer to Taking Corrective Action from Controlling a Stage process), however once pre-defined boundaries are crossed then the Project Board has to be involved.

PRINCE2 Processes (CP)

- Process CLOSING A PROJECT
  - De-commissioning a Project
  - Identifying Follow on Actions
  - Project Evaluation Review

Prince2 Community Forum: www.p2ug.com

PRINCE® is a registered trade mark of OGC (www.ogc.gov.uk)

By definition a project has to end !

NB – if a project doesn't have an end – then it is simply a set of operational activities

A clear end to a project will prevent spiralling costs and a perpetual merry-go-round effect. There can still be some incomplete activities at the end of a project – provided they are noted.

De-commissioning a Project – involves customer and supplier agreeing that the project delivered what was expected. Also advise suppliers of impending closure so that they can start to plan resource movements and compilation of all records for potential future audits or estimation exercises.

Identifying Follow on Actions – unfinished activities can be noted and assigned to operational management

Project Evaluation Review – the opportunity to capture the learning from the project, so that our next project can derive benefits.

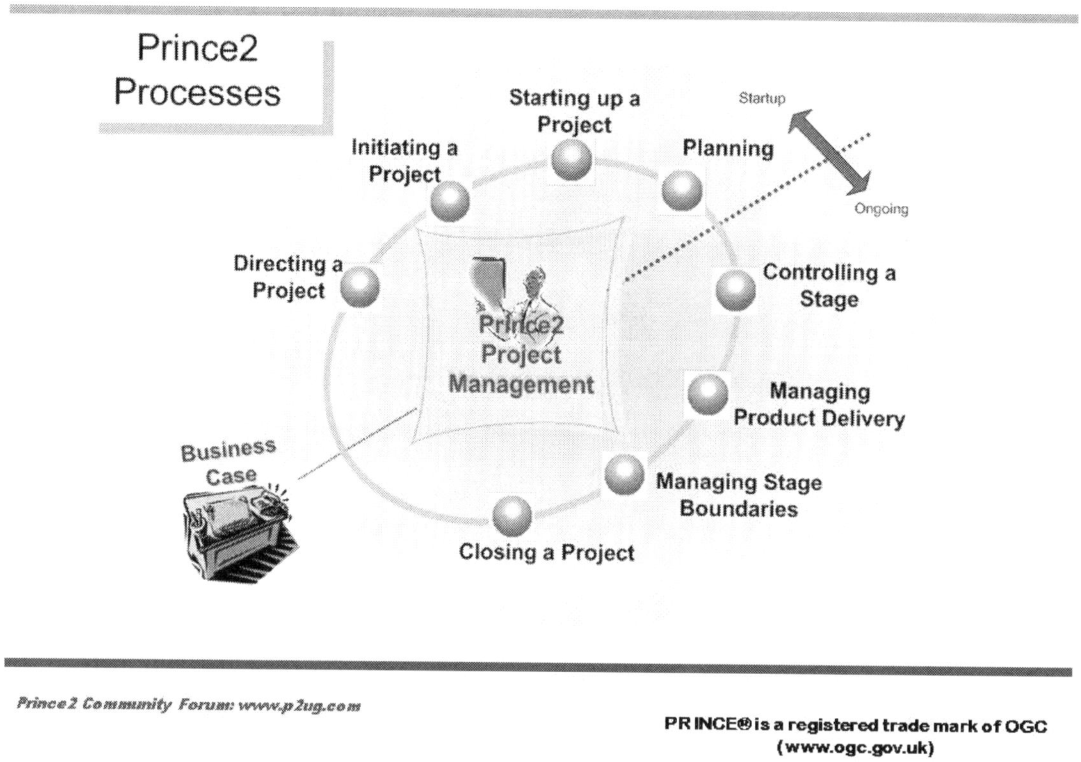

The circle diagram here also helps us understand that all processes require information from and provide information to other processes.

The processes define the management activities to be carried out during the project.

Introduction to PRINCE2 SUMMARY

- PRINCE is a structured project management methodology applicable to all types of projects
- PRINCE comprises of eight processes and eight supporting/influencing components
- Further information:
  - www.ogc.gov.uk/prince (the official PRINCE website)
  - www.p2ug.com (The PRINCE User Group)

IT SERVICE MANAGEMENT

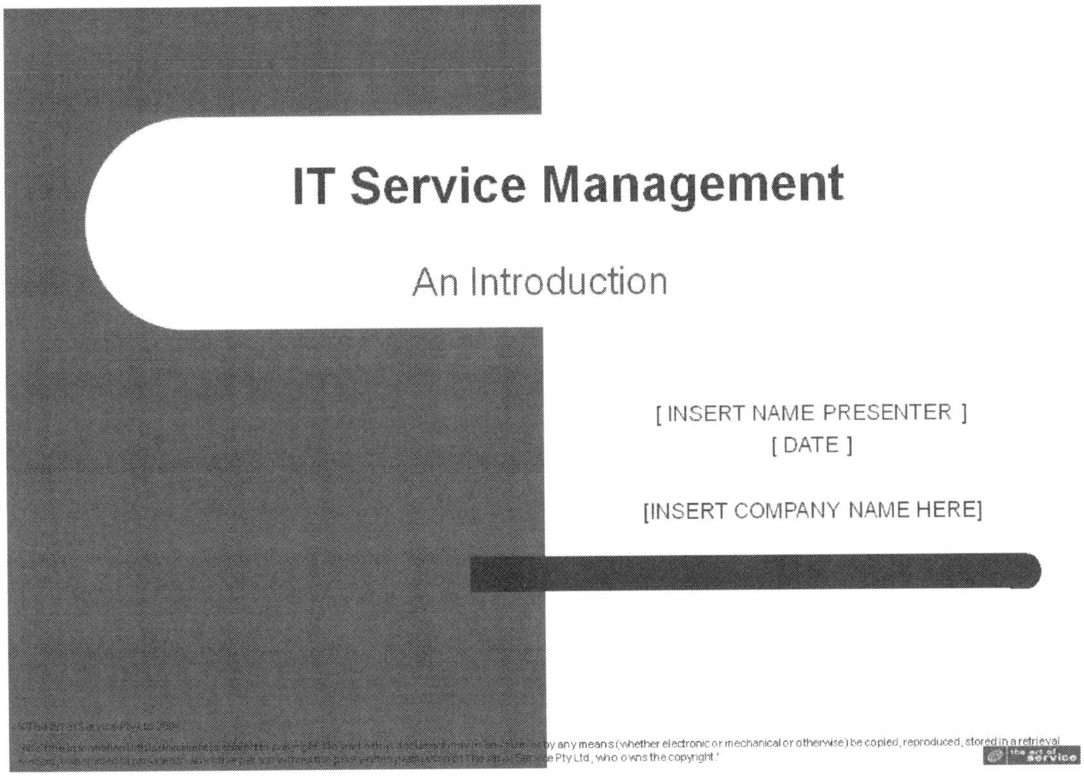

Please see Why – Service Level Management on page 101 within this workbook.

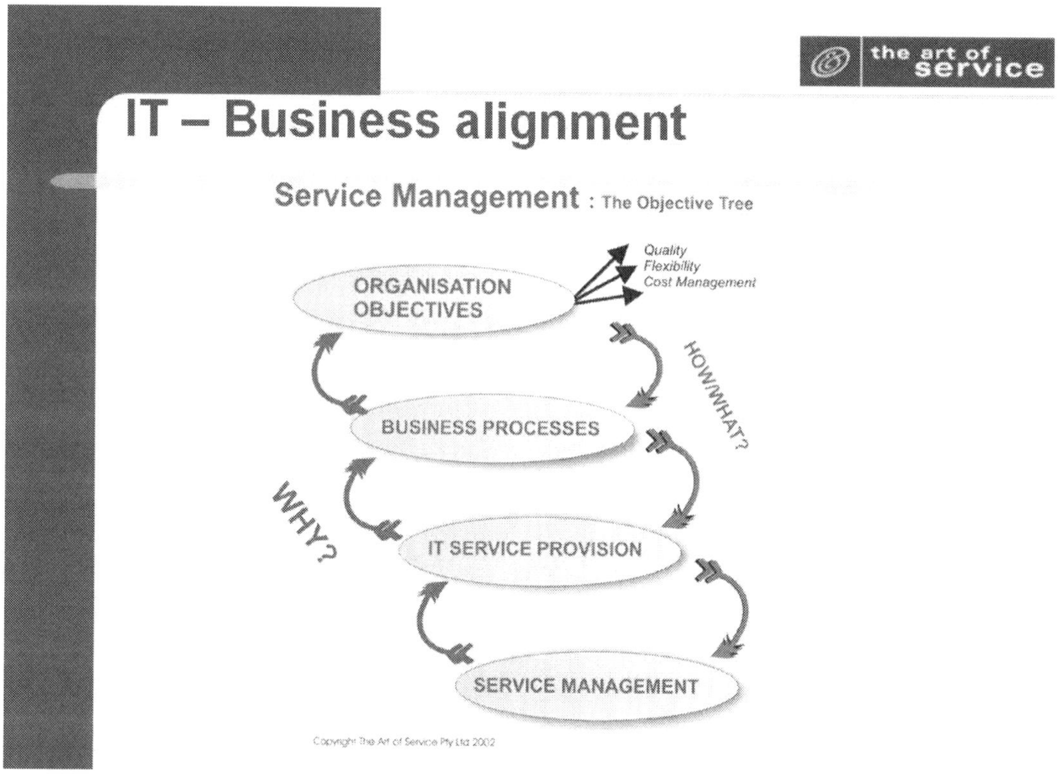

What is it that the business is in business for? Remember this is not about what the IT objectives or goals are, but what this organization seeks to achieve.
Remember the objectives of the business are only met through a series of activities involving a variety of different functional units – we call these business processes.

And… what about IT… do these business processes need IT services?
In what way does the IT group support the business and how is this visible?
The Services delivered by IT is what we refer to as IT Service Provision.
Service Management helps the IT group to provide effective and efficient services to the customer (customer is an ITIL term for the person that "pays for the service delivery)/end user according to their demands, needs and wishes.

This powerful, but simple concept really positions that requirement for the IT to business alignment. By looking at the tree downwards we understand what has to be done and how. By looking at the tree upwards we can understand why each component of the tree has to support the one component above it.

the art of service

Top ten concerns of IT Directors

1. Aligning IT strategy with business strategy
2. Meeting business and user needs
3. Coping with change
4. Dealing with senior management
5. Managing costs, budgets and resources
6. Keeping up with technology
7. Recruiting and retaining staff
8. Time and resource management
9. Infrastructure management
10. Maintaining skills and knowledge

This list is intended to almost be a comical one for most people involved in IT. Most times when you are presenting you will get agreement from the participants that in fact these are the things that require improvement.
The list is generic, but the fundamentals regarding the concerns are the same the world over.

It is also a list of things that IT Service Management principles guided by the ITIL Framework will help to address.

If these are of NO concern to you, there is a fair chance that you won't need IT Service Management and the ITIL Framework. However, if your participants state that these aren't a concern spend a bit of time talking to them and you will most likely uncover some of these issues.

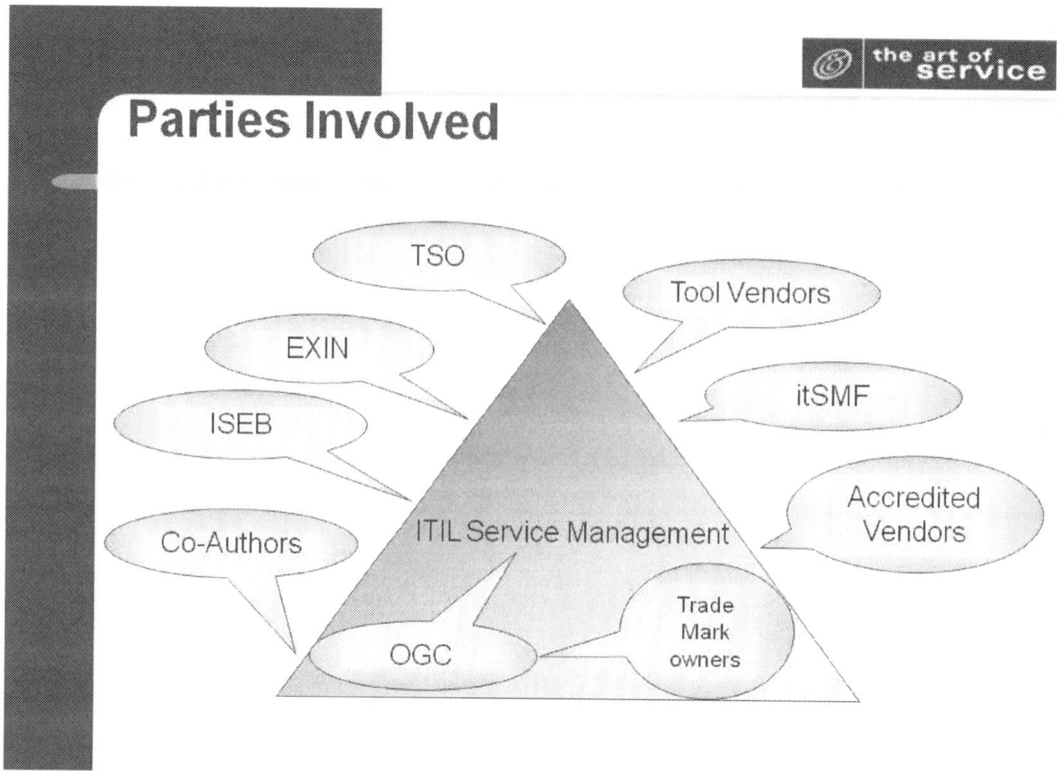

Explain that the Office of Government Commerce (OGC) are the copyright/trade mark owners of the ITIL Framework. The ITIL Framework are written with input from a variety of authors.

Explain about EXIN; they take care of exams (as does ISEB) – setting exams and marking.
This certification is recognized worldwide and the ITIL Foundations exams can be taken at Prometric Test Centers and other testing locations.

itSMF – global user group for those interested in IT Service Management and ITIL
TSO – The Stationary Office – publishers of the ITIL Text books and CD materials.
Accredited vendors offer training and consultancy services concerned with ITIL. The "accreditation" comes from EXIN or ISEB
Co-authors – develop the ITIL material (from large and small organizations around the world – but generally with a heavy emphasis on people from Europe)

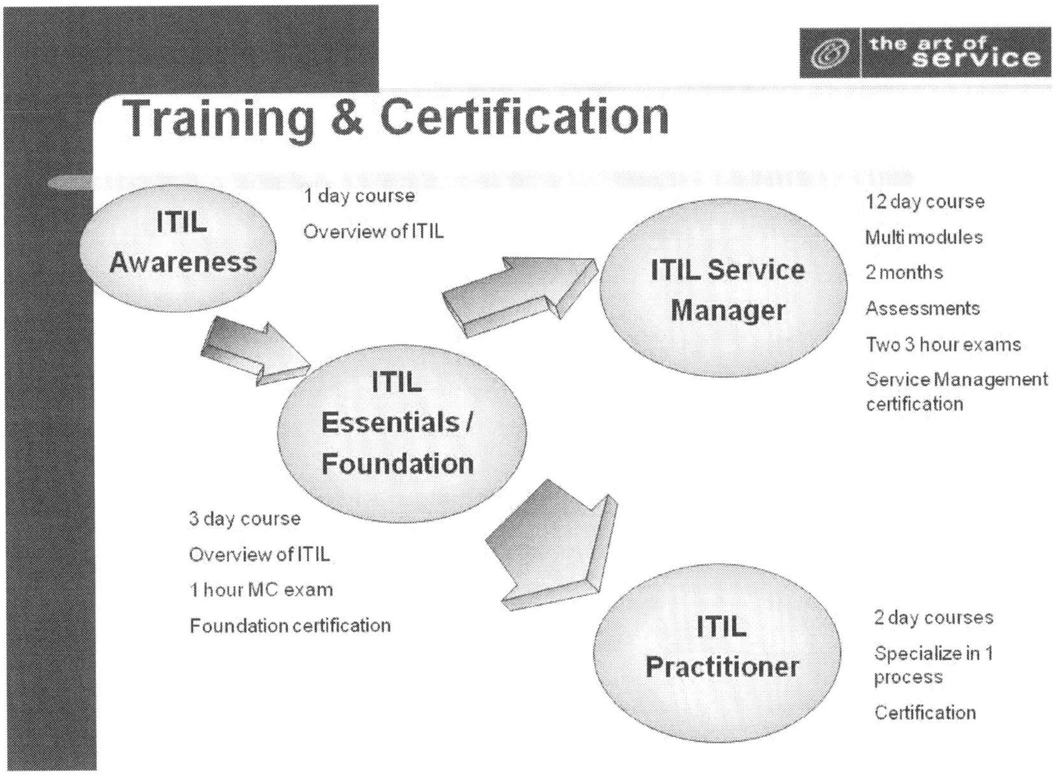

For those who are interested… the training options!

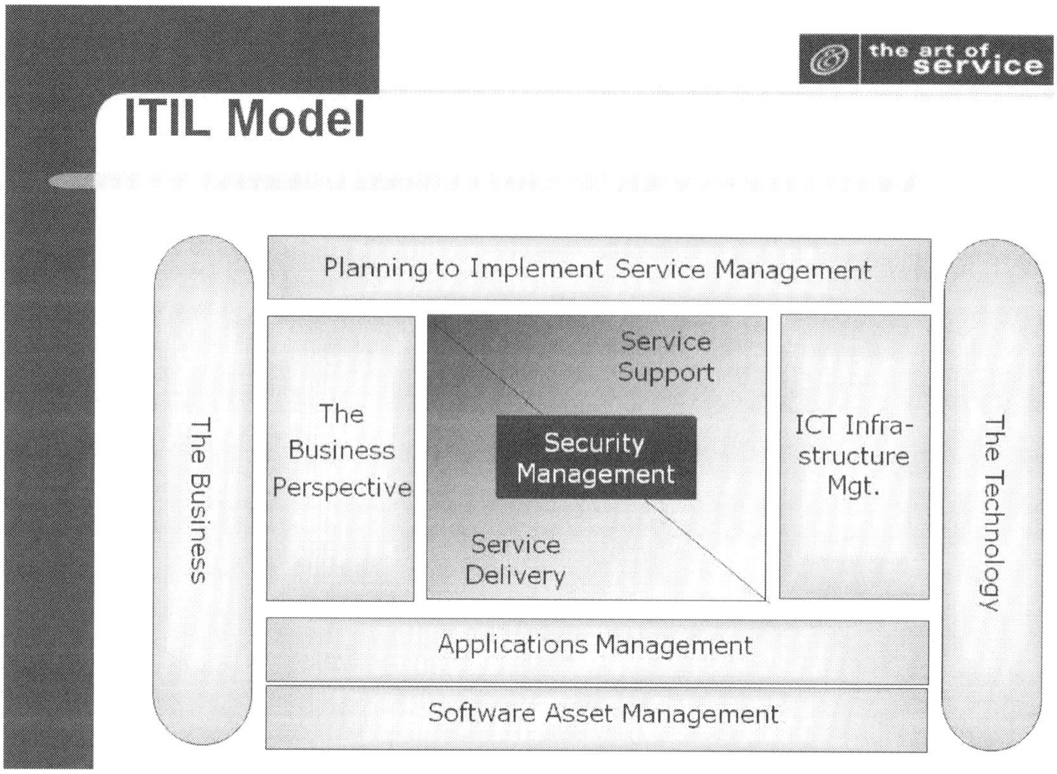

At the time of writing there are actually 8 core components of the ITIL Framework.
The names of the publications are shown here.

Show how the publications form a natural bridge between the business and the technology of the business.

What I like about this itSMF model is that it shows the business and the technology perspective. All the different areas are represented by different books. Security management is in the middle, as it is a vital process (officially, not part of service support or delivery).

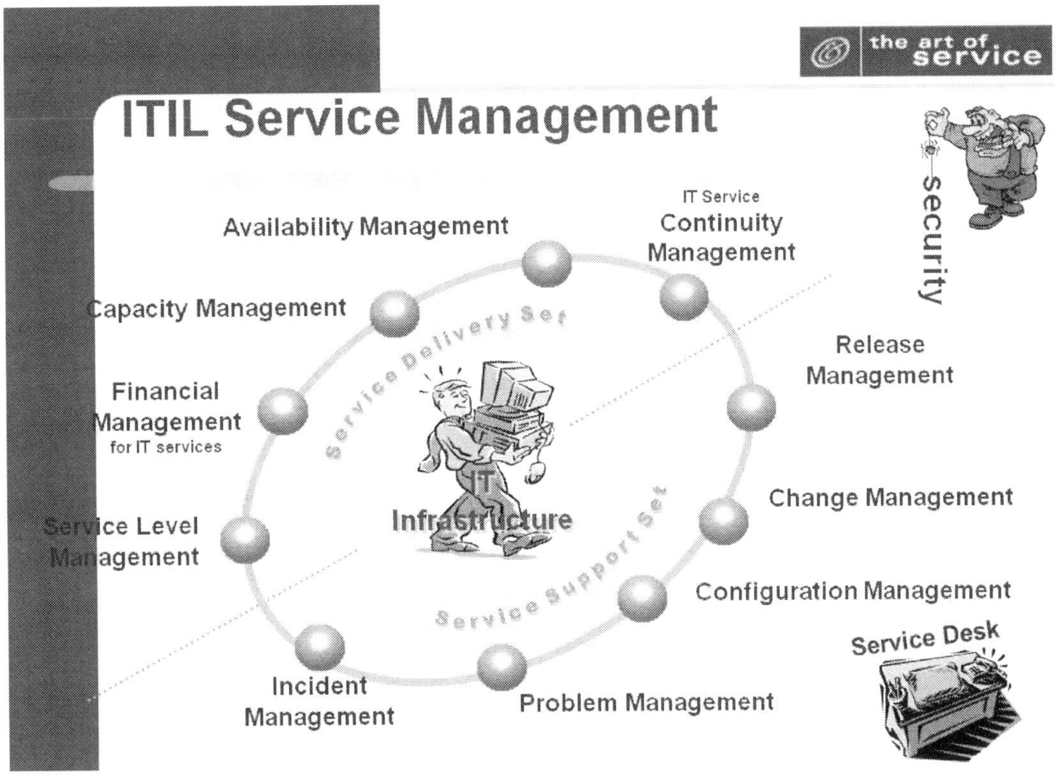

This diagram is a very powerful and easy to understand representation of the 10 processes and Service Desk Function that are covered in the Service Support and Service Delivery publications.

Use this slide to show how each of the process names are common sense and a lot of the concepts will already be known and understood by the participants.

What ITIL does offer is a well structured definition of each of these process areas, along with the inter-relationships between each of the processes.

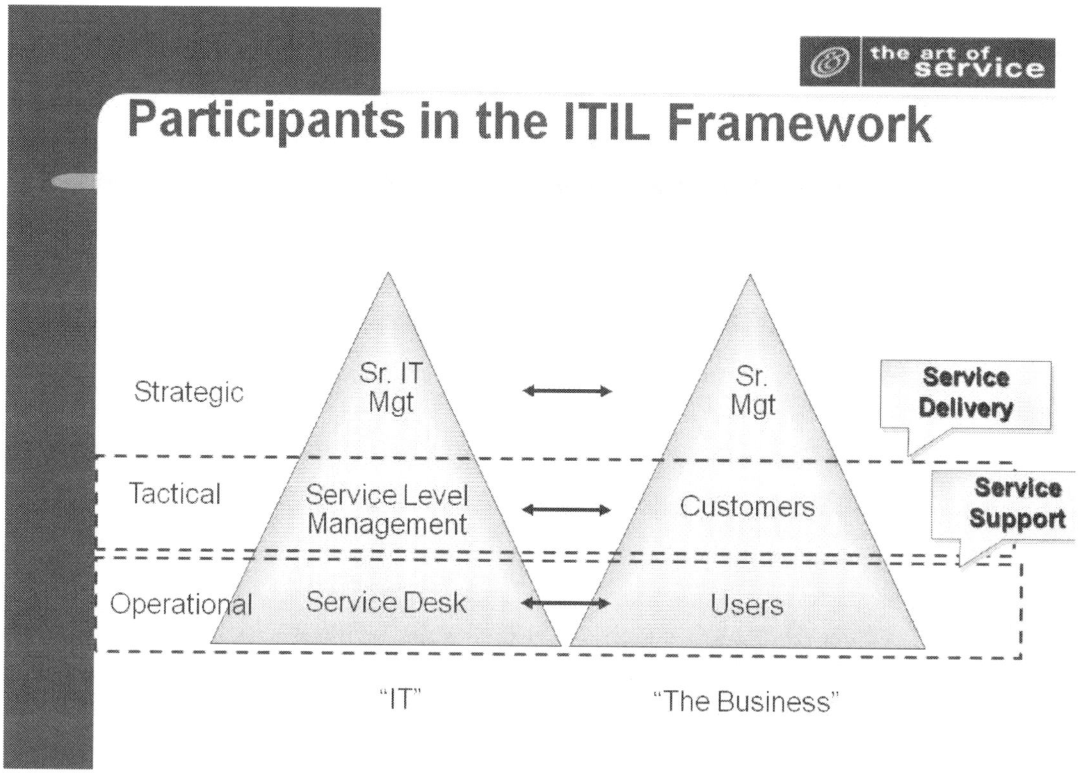

Explain the difference between operational, tactical and strategic activities.

•Operational activities can be considered as day-to-day activities.
•Tactical activities are designed to ensure that the strategic direction is translated into a service that can be operationally supported and reflects the customer requirements.

Difference between end users and customers…
•users make use of the IT services
•customers pay for it.

Senior management sets policy and ensures strategies and goals are aligned.

This is to show that they are all part of the ITIL activities

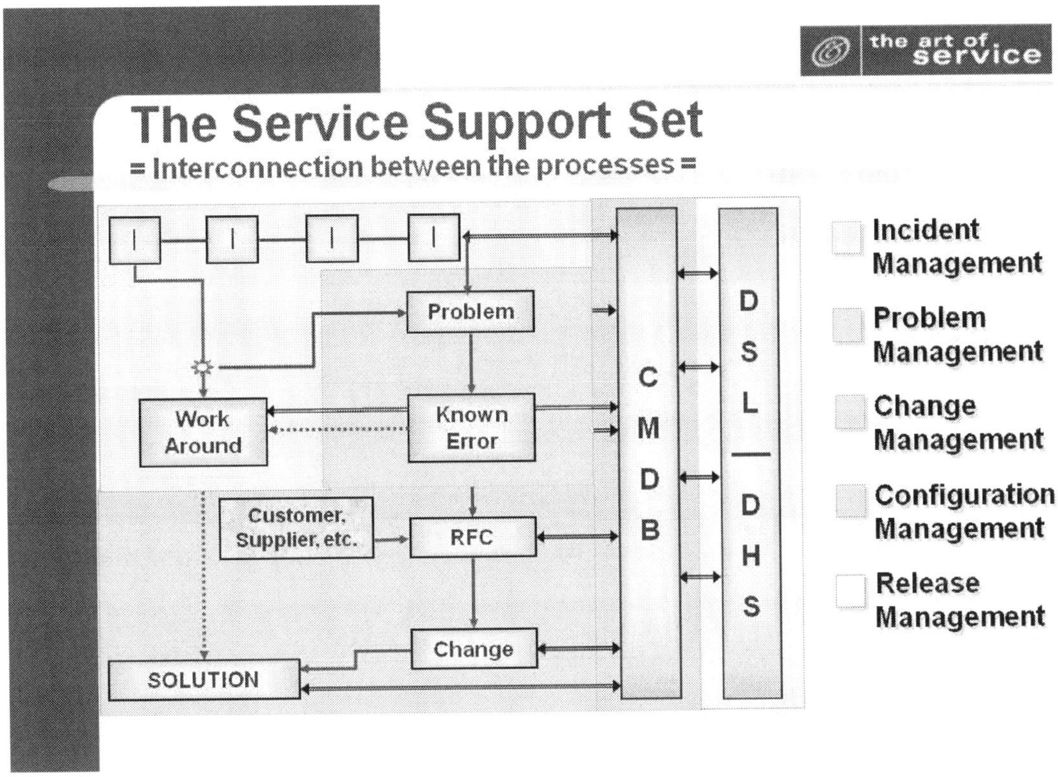

This slide shows the Service Support processes in a nutshell.

From this slide you get to see that while ITIL defines very good stand alone processes, the real benefit in the framework is the close inter-process relationships.

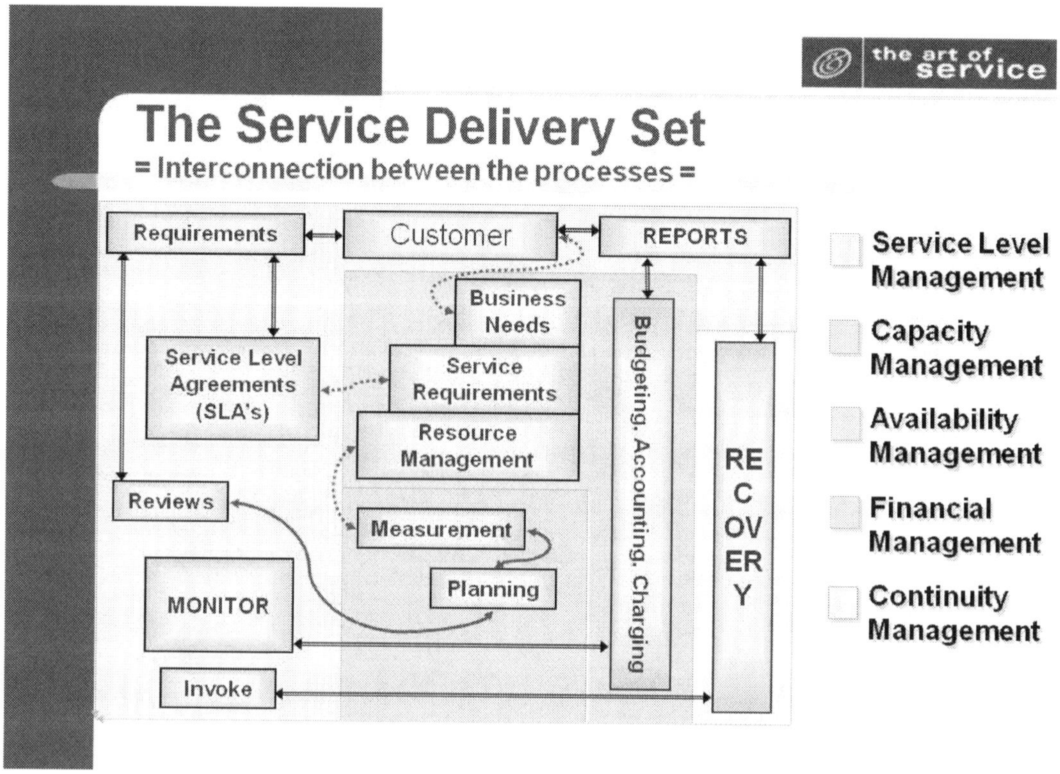

Service Delivery processes in a nutshell.

From this slide you get to see that while ITIL defines very good stand alone processes, the real benefit in the framework is the close inter-process relationships.

SUPPORTING DOCUMENTS

Through the documents, look for text surrounded by << and >> these are indicators for you to create some specific text.

Watch also for highlighted text which provides further guidance and instructions.

PROJECT SUPPORT ROLE DESCRIPTION

The Project Support role is optional within the Prince2 method of Project Management.

It is a role that could be utilized to perform some of the process supporting components. For example, the role could undertake the Configuration Management activity – which is typically a time consuming task for the Project Manager.

Another crucial area of support is the Change Control and/or provision of expert advice on specialist topics.

Responsibilities of the Project Support role

- Provide assistance to under resourced teams
- Act as a secondary Project Manager in case of absence
- Consult and advise on theoretical issues (e.g. Prince2 practices)
- Project filing – establish and manage
- Manage document control system
- Report compilation, preparation, presentation
- Review of plans (activities review, time frames review, costs review)
- Chair Quality review meetings
- Capture the expected outcomes from meetings
- Review time sheets and logs of work completed for accuracy and completeness of information

PRINCE 2 FACT SHEET

PRINCE® is a registered trade mark of OGC

History

Prince came into being in 1989, after work from the UK Governments CCTA – now called the Office of Government Commerce (OGC). Prince was originally based on another method called "PROMPT" (from Simpact Systems Ltd (1975).

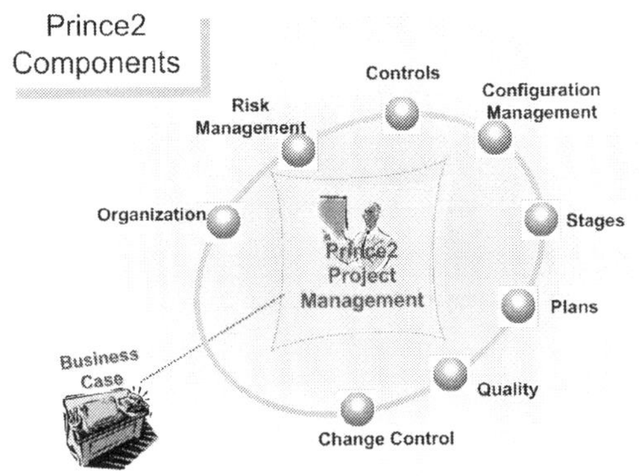

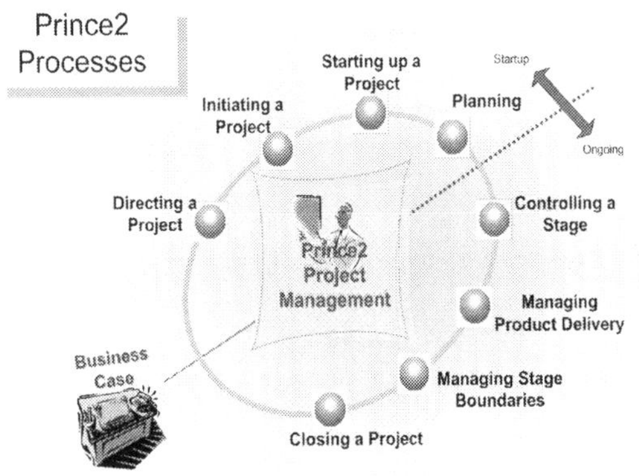

Structure

The structure of Prince2 is brilliantly simple. There are 8 considerations that have to be thought of with regard to the entire project (called "components"), then there are 8 processes that map out the required activities for each project. Throw in role definitions and there you have it.

Principle Concepts

Principle concepts are the things you need to remember if you want to demonstrate you have an understanding of Prince2.

Principle concepts for Prince2 are:

1. Customer and Supplier. Customer pays for the project. Supplier delivers the project. Suppliers can be external or internal to the organization.
2. Products. Prince2 focuses on the delivery of products. Products are measurable deliverables.

3. Stages. Prince2 projects are split into several stages to allow easier control, measurement and management.
4. Program Management versus Project Management. Prince2 recognizes that one project may be part of an overall Program of projects. This is taken into account.

Ownership and Education

Prince2 belongs to the Office of Government Commerce (OGC), in the UK. The OGC also own the ITIL (IT Infrastructure Library). There are some obvious links between ITIL and Prince2. In terms of Prince2 qualifications. There is the Foundation and the Practitioner.

Role Definitions

<u>Project Management Team</u>

Project Board	Represents (at management level) the organization
Executive	Ultimate accountability for the project, focus on return on investment
Senior User	Represents the users and makes sure that the products to be delivered are clearly defined and fit for purpose when they are delivered.
Senior Supplier	Has a focus on delivering the requirements of the Senior User (within typical constraints)
Project Manager	Day-to-day management of the project
Team Leader	An optional role, where teams of specialists are used on specific products/activities then the Project Manager may require a Single Point of Contact
Project Assurance	The Project Board need an assurance that the project is going according to the reports they will receive from the Project Manager
Project Support	Optional, administrative support for the Project Manager

PROGRAM MANGER ROLE DESCRIPTION

The Program Organization Team

The program organization is a separate entity from the Project Team. The Program team is formed in instances where an organization has multiple projects or has ongoing projects that should follow a similar method.
A business can have many Projects. Only one Program Organization should exist.

Role description: Program Manager

The Program Manager is the equivalent of the Project Manager but at the Program level. The Program Manager is the day-to-day representative of the Program Director (the Project Manager is the day-to-day representative of the Project Board).

A key requirement for the role is to understand the relationships between all projects. Through this understanding the Program Manager can assess flow on effect changes in one project to others. This is crucial for the assessment of shared risks, changes in business strategy and any requirement the business may have to reduce project, when looking for cost reduction.
Responsibilities of the Program Manger role.

Review and analyze the project risks and the flow on effect of risks
Ensure Project Boards and Project Managers communicate in a way that will improve the likelihood of project success and reduce the duplication of effort.
Make decisions regarding changes to resource requirements, altered priorities and management of exceptions.

PROJECT MANAGER ROLE DESCRIPTION

The Project Management Team

Role description: Project Manager

The Project Manager has the authority to run the project on a day-to-day basis. This role is the "on the ground" representative of the Project Board.

The role takes direction from the Project Board regarding issues relating to costs, timeframes and deliverables (products).

The Project Manager is responsible for producing the products that will deliver the benefits specified in the Project Initiation Document (PID).

Responsibilities of the Project Manager

- Prepare the project, stage (and possibly) exception reports for the Project Board
- Take responsibility for the production of required products
- Direct Team member activities
- Coordinate with Program Management if applicable
- Monitor project progress and results
- Delegate any project assurance role required by the Project Board
- Review and monitor risks to the project
- Prepare risk management strategies and plans in case of a risk eventuating
- Communicate and liaise with users and suppliers

PLAN AND PROJECT

Title

Quality Plan and Project Handbook

Author

<<Author Name>>

Search on << or >>… you need to fill in details between these marks.. also search on mm/dd/yyyy.

Version

x.x

Version Date

<<Date Details>>

Version

<<Draft/Revision/Final>>

Revision History

Date	Author	Revision	Description of Change
mm/dd/yyyy	<< >>	x.x	Preliminary issue (First draft)
mm/dd/yyyy	<< >>	x.x	<<Comments>>
mm/dd/yyyy	<< >>	x.x.x	<<Comments>>

Purpose of the Project Management Plan

The purposes of this Project Management Plan are the following:

- instill a sense of user confidence in the quality of the work that the Project Team will perform by showing how the project will be carried out, measured, monitored, accounted for and safeguarded during and after development,
- define roles and responsibilities, with emphasis on the required skill sets to address the complexities and risks of the project,
- show how changes and problems can be identified and reported,
- clearly define the content, format, sign-off and review process, and responsibilities for each deliverable,
- make visible all the means that are and will be applied to meet the user's technical and quality requirements,
- provide the supplier's quality authority with information that allows him to organize quality assurance and quality control activities that include transfer of information, verification actions, etc.,
- state all the participants of the project, procedures, rules and applicable methods.

In sort, this Project Plan provides a definition of the project, including goals and objectives. It is a contract between the Project Manager, Executive Sponsor, Project Team and other management of the consortium with and/or affected by the project. The project plan provides the baseline against which to monitor project costs and project progress stage by stage. It identifies key deliverables, resource requirements, total costs and control points.

Background Information

mm/dd/yyyy <<e.g. Call for tenders issued>>
mm/dd/yyyy <<e.g. Participants submit bid>>
mm/dd/yyyy <<e.g. Selection Process>>
mm/dd/yyyy <<e.g. Negotiations with selected partner>>
mm/dd/yyyy <<e.g. Milestone date – Contract signed>>

mm/dd/yyyy the negotiations started with <<selected vendor/Consortium>>

- <<if Consortium – Vendor 1>>
- <<if Consortium – Vendor 2>>

- <<if Consortium – Vendor 3>>
- <<if Consortium – Vendor x>>

mm/dd/yyyy work allocation is modified and <<selected vendor/Consortium member>> retains the management of the project (<<PROJECT SHORT NAME>>) whilst <<SELECTED VENDOR/CONSORTIUM MEMBER>> undertakes the person months previously allocated to <<SELECTED VENDOR/CONSORTIUM MEMBER>> in all other WPs.
mm/dd/yyyy The contract was signed by <<SELECTED VENDOR/CONSORTIUM MEMBER>> in <<city>>.
mm/dd/yyyy the contract was signed by the Commission. Start date of the project is mm/dd/yyyy.

Field of application - Scope

Scope is the way that we describe the boundaries of the project. It defines what the project will deliver and what it will not deliver.
We consider that a clear and concise definition of scope is key to the success of the **<<project name>>** project. In this section we describe, from a quantitative perspective, what is to be accomplished, in order to create realistic work plans, budgets, schedules, and expectations. If the identified work falls outside the defined scope, the Project Manager shall either deem the work out of scope and defer it, or expand the scope of the project to include the work. The latter choice would result in formal changes to the work plan, resource allocation, budget and/or schedule.

Scope Definition

The scope of the project is defined through its goals, which for **<<project name>>** are:

- <<Project Goal 1>>
- <<Project Goal 2>>
- <<Project Goal x>>

The main functionality that the **<<project name>>** system will support is:

- <<Functionality Statement 1>>
- <<Functionality Statement 2>>
- << Functionality Statement x>>

Costs

The final cost of the project should not exceed the cost stated in the Contract.

Benefits

Benefits as expressed in contract must be respected at the maximum extend.

Risks

Each risk type is described in Risk Management plan. For each risk, the cost of the event is determined and the likelihood that the event might occur. The mitigation Strategy states how you the impact of each risk event is planned to be diminished (mitigation).

References and applicable documents

Reference documents are documents which:

- Are explicitly mentioned in the text of the Project Management Plan
- Do not contain binding requirements

Applicable documents are those documents which:

- May not be explicitly mentioned in the Project Management Plan (other than here)
- Contain binding requirements for the project (requirement that must be fulfilled and for which satisfaction may be verified)

Reference documents

No	Name	Reference	Ref.No
1.	**<<project name>>** <<short description>>	<<reference>>	<<number>>

Applicable documents

No	Name	Reference	Ref. No
1	<<e.g. Selected vendor/Consortium>> Agreement	Appendix <<a>>	<<x>>1
2	<<e.g. Memorandum of Understanding with relevant parties>>	Appendix <<b>>	<<x>>2
3	<<e.g. Configuration Management Plan>>	Appendix <<c>>	<<x>>3
4	<<e.g. Change Management Plan>>	Appendix <<d>>	<<x>>4
5	<<e.g. Communications Plan>>	Appendix <<e>>	<<x>>5
6	<<e.g. Risk Management Plan>>	Appendix <<f>>	<<x>>6
7	<<e.g. Project Time Plan>>	Appendix <<g>>	<<x>>7

Terminology

Abbreviations and acronyms

No	Abbr/Acr	Description
1.	PO	Project Officer
2.	PM	Project Manager
3.	PCB	Project Coordination Board
4.	PMP	Project management Plan
5.	ADD	Architectural Design Document
6.	ATP	Acceptance Test Plan
7.	ATR	Acceptance Test Report
8.	DDD	Detailed Design Document
9.	MMM	Minutes of Monthly Meetings
10.	MPR	Monthly Project Progress Report
11.	OPM	Operations Manual
12.	PAF	Pre-analysis and Feasibility Report

13.	PAR	Pre-analysis Report
14.	PPR	Project Progress Report
15.	PRA	Project Audit Report
16.	QAR	Project Quality Audit Report
17.	QCR	Quality Control Report
18.	SIR	Site Installation Report
19.	TRR	Technical Review Report
20.	URS	User Requirements Specifications

Presentation of the project - General presentation

Project Goals and Objectives

The aim of the proposed project is to design, implement and validate an **<<project name>>** that will exhibit the following characteristics:

- <<required characteristic 1>>
- <<required characteristic 2>>
    - <<required sub-characteristic 2.1>>
    - <<required sub-characteristic 2.2>>
- <<required characteristic x>>

Benefits to the participants

In addition to the financial benefits that all partners will enjoy as stakeholders of the **<<project name>>** each of them will also experience alternative benefits.

- <<Project Benefit 1>>
- <<Project Benefit 2>>
- <<Project Benefit x>>

<<Project Benefit 1 expansion>>

<<Expansion on stated benefit for the project>>.

<<Project Benefit 2 expansion>>

<<Expansion on stated benefit for the project>>.

<<Project Benefit x expansion>>

<<Expansion on stated benefit for the project>>.

Deliverables

Business Deliverables

Del. ID	Deliverable name	WP	Who	Contractual Deliverable	Deliverable Type [1]	Delivery (project month)
D3.1	<<deliverable name>>	WPx	**<<SELECTED VENDOR/CONSORTIUM MEMBER>>**	y/n	Report	x
D3.2	<<deliverable name>>	WPx	**<<SELECTED VENDOR/CONSORTIUM MEMBER>>**	y/n	Report	x
D3.3	<<deliverable name>>	WPx	**<<SELECTED VENDOR/CONSORTIUM MEMBER>>**	y/n	Report	x
D3.4	<<deliverable name>>	WPx	**<<SELECTED VENDOR/CONSORTIUM MEMBER>>**	y/n	Report	x
D4.1	<<deliverable name>>	WPx	**<<SELECTED VENDOR/CONSORTIUM MEMBER>>**	y/n	Specification	x
D4.2	<<deliverable name>>	WPx	**<<SELECTED VENDOR/CONSORTIUM MEMBER>>**	y/n	Specification	x
D4.3	<<deliverable name>>	WPx	**<<SELECTED VENDOR/CONSORTIUM MEMBER>>**	y/n	Specification	xx
D5	<<deliverable name>>	WPx	**<<SELECTED VENDOR/CONSORTIUM MEMBER>>**	y/n	Report	xx
D6.1	<<deliverable name>>	WPx	**<<SELECTED VENDOR/CONSORTIUM MEMBER>>**	y/n	Specification/Prototype	xx
D6.2	<<deliverable name>>	WPx	**<<SELECTED VENDOR/CONSORTIUM MEMBER>>**	y/n	Specification/Prototype	xx
D6.3	<<deliverable name>>	WPx	**<<SELECTED VENDOR/CONSORTIUM MEMBER>>**	y/n	Specification/System	xx

[1] A short, self-evident description e.g. report, demonstration, conference, specification, prototype...

Project Deliverables

Del. ID	Deliverable name	WP	Leading partner	Contractual Deliverable	Deliverable Type [2]	Delivery (project month)
D1.1	<<deliverable name>>	<<PROJECT SHORT NAME>>	**<<SELECTED VENDOR/CONSORTIUM MEMBER>>**	y/n	Contract	x
D1.2	<<deliverable name>>	<<PROJECT SHORT NAME>>	**<<SELECTED VENDOR/CONSORTIUM MEMBER>>**	y/n	Report	X
D1.3	<<deliverable name>>	<<PROJECT SHORT NAME>>	**<<SELECTED VENDOR/CONSORTIUM MEMBER>>**	y/n	Report	Xx
D1.4	Final Project Report	<<PROJECT SHORT NAME>>	**<<SELECTED VENDOR/CONSORTIUM MEMBER>>**	y/n	Report	xx
D1.X	Bimonthly Progress Report	<<PROJECT SHORT NAME>>	**<<SELECTED VENDOR/CONSORTIUM MEMBER>>**	Y	Report	Every other month
D2	Dissemination and Use Plan	WP2	**<<SELECTED VENDOR/CONSORTIUM MEMBER>>**	Y	Report	6

Division into work units

Contractual work units

WP	Work Package title	Work Description	Effort (man-months)	Deadline (project month)
<<PROJECT SHORT NAME>>	Project Management	This work package will provide the appropriate project management support infrastructure.	xx	xx
WP x	<<title>>	<<description>>	xx	xx
WP x	User Requirements and Specifications of the **<<project name>>** Services	This work package will identify and document in an iterative manner the requirements of the different “participants” involved in the **<<project name>>**. Following that it will identify the required system attributes and specify the services to be offered by the **<<project name>>** system for each participant type.	xx	xx
WP x	Functional Specification and	During this work package the architectural model and system	xx	xx

[2] A short, self-evident description e.g. report, demonstration, conference, specification, prototype...

	System Architecture	functionality required for satisfying the User Requirements, will be specified in an iterative manner		
WP x	Quality Strategy	This work package will specify the quality components, as well as methods for monitoring them, which will be used during the **<<project name>>** development, evaluation and demonstration stages. Furthermore, it will specify the procedures that will be adopted for ensuring interoperability between the various system components and modules.	xx	xx
WP x	Technical Design and System Implementation	During this Work package the functional specifications of the **<<project name>>** service platform and its associated application modules, will be utilized for the technical design, implementation and initial testing of an electronic **<<project name>>** system simulating, over the Internet, the existing **<<project name>>** processes.	xx	xx
WP x	<<title>>	<<description>>	xx	xx
WP x	<<title>>	<<description>>	xx	xx
WP x	<<title>>	<<description>>	xx	xx

Work breakdown

The work breakdown, which includes a listing of the refined units of work within each of the contractual higher level ones, will be found in the subsequent contractual deliverable D1.2 –Detailed Project plan.

For each refined unit of work a description will be given together with an estimation of its deadlines, the person effort required and the necessary resources.

Project Time Plan

At this stage the project time plan, which has been prepared and can be found in Appendix G, has been based on the contractual requirements as far as work units, deadlines and resources are concerned.

However it goes beyond this level by incorporating more refined units of work based on the project milestones, for which both resources and effort time has been allocated.

This plan will be updated and refined as a result of the detailed planning work that will subsequently be performed and will be included in the contractual deliverable - Detailed Project plan.

Project Organization and Responsibilities

We provide an organization chart with the roles you described below.

Role-Title	Name	Company/Organization.
Project Manager(*)	<<name 1>>	**<<SELECTED VENDOR/CONSORTIUM MEMBER>>**
Operations Manager	<<name 2>>	**<<SELECTED VENDOR/CONSORTIUM MEMBER>>**
Technical Coordinator	<<name 3>>	**<<SELECTED VENDOR/CONSORTIUM MEMBER>>**
Quality Assurance Coordinator	<<name x>>	**<<SELECTED VENDOR/CONSORTIUM MEMBER>>**

Any change of the Supplier's Key personnel marked with a asterisk (*) shall be subject to written agreement

Involved parties and their roles

Partner	Principal Role
<<selected vendor/Consortium member>>	Project Management <<further description>>
<<selected vendor/Consortium member>>	Technical/ Quality and Reliability Analysis of new User Requirements, Technical Design & System Implementation <<further description>>
<<selected vendor/Consortium member>>	Monitoring of the System's Security Aspects <<further description>>
<<selected vendor/Consortium member>>	Maintenance of the system's Quality, Aspects Analysis of new User Requirements <<further description>>
<<selected vendor/Consortium member>>	Planning of new on-line administration services, Dissemination Activities <<further description>>

Organization of the project teams

PROJECT ORGANIZATION LAYERS		
Layer	Task	Role
1	Direction of the project	PCB
2	Day-to-day Management	Project Manager
3	Team Management	WP Leader
4	Work to create deliverables	Team Members

Responsibilities

Project Coordination Board (PCB).

A senior member from each partner together with the project manager, the operation manager and the technical and QA coordinators will form the project coordination board (PCB). The scope of the PCB is to represent the interests and objectives of each partner and to take all project decisions.

The *Parties* shall establish, within <<xx>> days after the date of this *Consortium Agreement*, the *PCB* composed of <<one/two/xx>> duly authorized representative of each of them.

After having informed the others in writing, each *Party* shall have the right to replace its representative and/or to appoint a proxy although it shall use all reasonable endeavors to maintain the continuity of its representation.

Each representative shall have a deputy. The deputy shall replace the representative in his duties when he is absent or he is unable to perform those duties.

Each partner shall have one vote in the PCB.

The *PCB* shall be chaired by <<PCB Chair>>.

Project Manager [PM]

Quality and Reliability International will appoint the project manager. His responsibilities include:

- Interact with the Commission for all project matters (contract, technical and financial issues, work plans, project deliverables, reviews etc)
- Monitor the progress of the project work and deliverable submission dates against the agreed milestones and work plan. Also ensure that the project scopes remain in line with the IST objectives.
- Co-ordinate all project activities through the operations manager, the technical co-coordinator and the QA co-coordinator.
- Maintain detailed financial and work effort records for each partner
- Communicate frequently with partners and establish links with other IST related projects.

Operations Manager [OM]

Will have the overall picture of the project operations and technical work, while he will be responsible for the key decisions regarding the project work and the overall operations direction.

Technical coordinator [TC]

Will be responsible to plan, monitor and report on all technical aspects of the project.

QA coordinator [QC]

Together with the project manager, will formulate and apply the project's quality plan and will lead the specification of the "**<<project name>>** Quality Strategy".

Work Package Leaders [WPL]

Will be responsible for planning, monitoring and reporting the technical work of the work package. In addition he/she will co-ordinate the partners involved in the specific work package and will take care of time schedules, all necessary progress reports and WP deliverables.

Site Project Managers [SPM]

Will be responsible (together with the user groups) for the day-to-day activities of the pilot sites and will monitor the progress of the project throughout its life-time. An important part of their role will be to ensure that the user requirements are communicated correctly, and that the WP leaders are aware of the acceptability and the user reactions on the services developed by the project.

Independent external evaluator [IEE]

Independent (not related to any member of the Consortium) physical person having no interests in **<<project name>>**, having the expertise and operations background, assigned to the role of Independent External Evaluator of the deliverables. The consortium assumes this person.

Escalation

The method to be followed for the escalation of problems encountered during the project is described in detail in the Change Management Plan

Subcontractors

((e.g. No subcontracting has been assigned up to now>>

Project Planning and Control

Plans

The major plans included in the Project Handbook are:

- Project Plan, see Appendix x
- Configuration management plan, see Appendix x
- Change management plan, see Appendix x
- Risk Management plan, see Appendix x
- Communications Plan, see Appendix x

Progress measurement and monitoring

Progress is measured by the MONTHLY REPORT FORM (see Configuration Management Plan). The PM makes a consolidation of the Monthly Reports of the Contributors and sends them to the PO.

Information about work progress

Progress reports

MONTHLY REPORT FORM are completed by the partners and sent by the 10th of month M+<<xx> to the PM.

Progress meetings

Progress meetings are organized within the context of WP teams and WP according to the needs at least once a week. The communications Plan defines these meetings and provides the required management framework see Appendix x

Acceptance Procedure and payment

The acceptance of deliverables and the reimbursement of eligible costs are implemented according to the contract.

Control of the Project Management Plan

Preparation

The Project Management Plan [PMP] is controlled by the Project Manger.

The Project Management Plan is continuously updated during the duration of the project.

Any changes to the project regarding schedule, cost, deliverables, roles etc they create a new version of the PMP or its Appendices. The PMP is stored to the **<<project name>>** web site. All participants are notified about PMP modifications by e-mail.

The reader may consult the Revision Information in order to be informed about last modifications.

Approval

The changes are approved by the Participants implicitly or explicitly.

Lack of adherence to Project Management Plan

The PM is responsible for the adherence of any action to the PMP. Any serious deviation is treated as a project issue by the PM and managed accordingly.

Plans

Configuration Management Plan

The fundamental purpose of Configuration Management (CM) is to establish and maintain the integrity and control of software products throughout a project's life cycle.

The Software Configuration Management process is comprised of the following integrated activities:

- Configuration identification of artifacts/ work products used or developed by a project
- Configuration change control of information, including the impact of changes to organizations, management practices, schedules, budgets, technical or assurance activities, testing or retest requirements, or project status

- Status accounting of artifacts / work products used in the development, release, and maintenance of a project
- Configuration reviews and audits that assess the status and acceptability of products controlled or released by CM.

The Full Configuration Management plan is presented in Appendix D

Change Management Plan

The issue of change the way it will be managed is incorporated in the Configuration Management Plan in Appendix x

Quality Management Plan

Contractual quality requirements

<<Contractual quality requirement 1>>:

<<Contractual quality requirement 1 description>>

<<Contractual quality requirement 2>>:

<<Contractual quality requirement 2 description>>

<<Contractual quality requirement x>>:

<<Contractual quality requirement x description>>

<<e.g. Accuracy:
Verifiability:
Security:
Convenience:
Flexibility:
Mobility:
Efficiency:
Scalability: >>

Appendices

Appendix x	Consortium Agreement
Appendix x	Memorandum of Understanding with Independent External Evaluators
Appendix x	<<project name>> Glossary
Appendix x	Configuration Management Plan
Appendix x	Communications Plan
Appendix x	Risk Management Plan
Appendix x	Project Time Plan

CHANGE MANAGER ROLE DESCRIPTION

The Program Organization Team

The program organization is a separate entity from the Project Team. The Program team is formed in instances where an organization has multiple projects or has ongoing projects that should follow a similar method.

A business can have many Projects. Only one Program Organization should exist.

Role description: Change Manager

The Change Manager is continually reviewing the 'business case' that has been the source document and justification for the Project funding.

The "change" that is being reviewed is related to the changes that will be required in the business – if and when the products delivered from a Project are available for deployment in the business.

Responsibilities of the Change Manager role
Review and make assessment on risks associated with adoption of project products in the business
Plan and manage a communication plan relating to impending changes
Educate business people on their required actions in order to take advantage of the changes that the project products will introduce
Ensure products are fully exploited in order to realize expected business benefits

Prince2 Roles

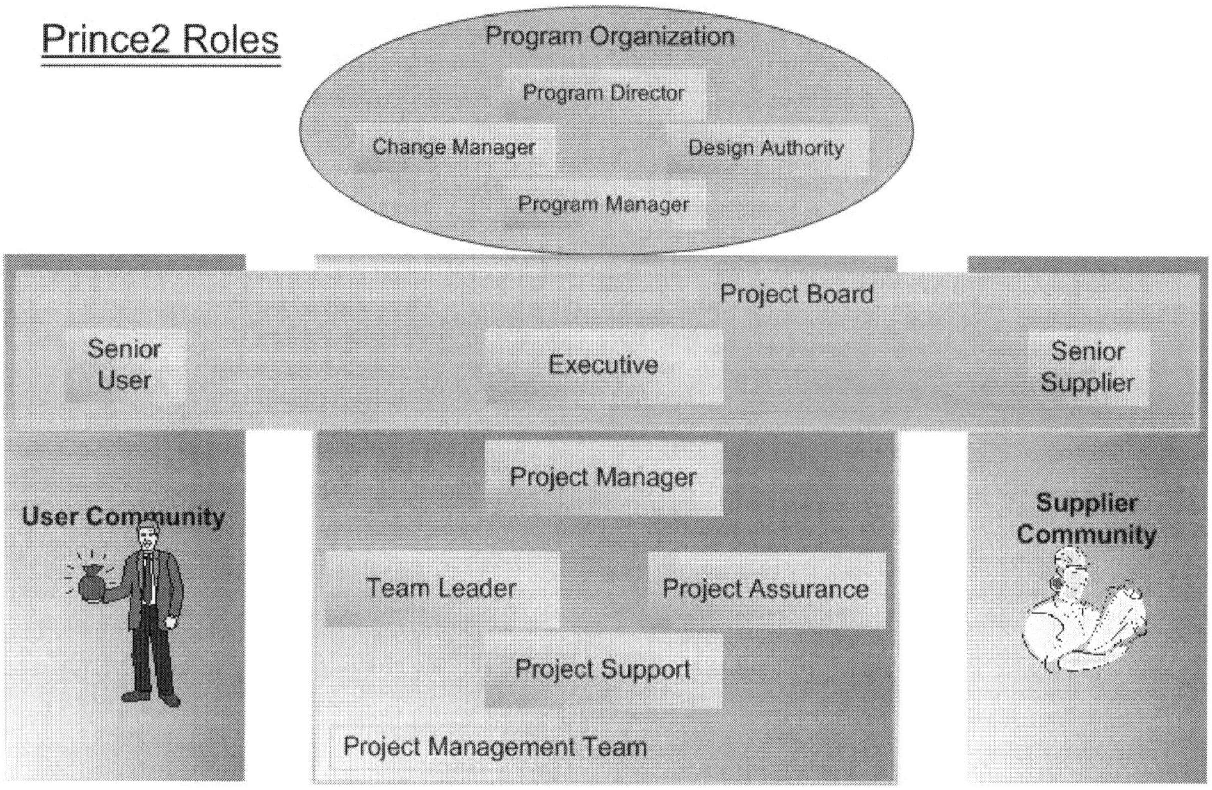

RISK ANALYSIS DOCUMENT

<<Organization name>>

Project: <<project Name>>
Initial Project Risks

Statu s:	In draft Under Review Sent for Approval Approved Rejected	
Versi on:	<<your version>>	
Rele ase Date:		

Document Control

Author

Prepared by <name and / or department>

Document Source

This document is located on the LAN under the path:

X:\ xxxx\Services/Project Management

Document Approval

This document has been approved for use by the following:

- <first name, last name>, Senior User
- <first name, last name>, Program Director (if applicable)
- <first name, last name>, Project Manager
- <first name, last name>, Project Board

Amendment History

Issue	Date	Amendments	Completed By

Distribution List

When this procedure is updated the following copyholders must be advised through email that an updated copy is available on the intranet site:

<Company Name> Business Unit	Stakeholders

Introduction

Purpose

The purpose of this document is to provide an overview of the known or expected risks for the <<project name>>.

Scope

This document describes the following:

- <<scope of document >> (the project name, the project scope).

Audience

This document is relevant to <<staff>> in <company name>

Ownership

<<Document Owner>> has ownership of this document.

Related Documentation

Include in this section any related reference numbers and other associated documentation:

Initial Project Risks

This document provides a template and examples of risks that face all projects during the initial phase and for the lifecycle of the project itself.

The reader is reminded of key issues, but will need to expand the template to suit their own expected risks, that comes as a result of experience in the field where the project is to be conducted.

Staffing Risks

- **Internal Resources** – The required staff will:-
  - Not be made sufficiently available
  - Not be at the required Business or expert level to meet the roles and responsibilities.

- **Testing resources** – The resources requirements for the testing activities would not be made available. Testing will need teams of up to five people for one-week periods. (Note: These activities are not funded for backfill)

- **Retention of Core Team throughout the duration of the project** - A major risk in any project is loss key people in the project team.

- **Core Team to remain "focused"** - The team may be diverted from the project to work on other short-term initiatives.

- **Identification, hiring and retention of experts** - Engaging the right people for the project team may:-
  - Take an unacceptable time period
  - Not be available
  - Cost more than the budget has allowed
    - IT/applications systems expert
    - Data conversion
    - Testing
    - Change Management
    - Project Administration

Organization / Change Risks

- Introduction of Change - The << COMPANY NAME >> organization will not be able to adopt the rate of change required by the Project.
    - Culture
    - Policies & Procedures
    - Customer relations
    - Attitudes
    - Disciplines
    - Processes
    - Interfaces
    - Industrial Relations
    - Health & Safety

- **Concurrent Implementation of Modules** - Implementing System modules concurrently is recognized as a "Risk contributor". When modules are implemented concurrently rather than sequentially: it causes a high drain on resources and may impact the day to day business and/or the project schedule.

- **BPR + System change** – Implementing Automation/Systems change simultaneously with Business Process Re-engineering (or change to Policies and Procedures) is recognized as a "Risk contributor".
  The high level functional processes needed to provide input to the new systems; have not yet been developed or tested. The business Models developed may be entirely suitable to support the requirements of our Multi vendor Service environment.

- **Executive direction** - The high level direction, goals and Policies & Procedures (Enterprise Model) may not be of sufficient detail to provide the necessary framework required by the detailed Business analysis.

- **Customer acceptance of the system** – Some customers may not accept the new system functionality or timetable.

- **Acceptance of Change** – The internal users of the systems may not fully and enthusiastically accept the changes in processes and the necessary disciplines.

- **Operational Management level** – The senior operational management layer (Logistics Manager, Overall Field Service Operations Manager, Marketing / Sales Manager and IT Manager) is missing. This may cause a loss of leadership and authority in the functional divisions and cause the old ways disciplines and processes to remerge. Each major system module and its associated data; need a functional "owner".

- **Major Organizational changes** - Major Organizational changes made during a project of this size introduce risk.

- **Functional leaders** - If the Project leaders are not full time and fully committed to the Project deliverables.

  The core team members of the project team must be dedicated to the project on a top priority basis. These project leaders must be the "Business Champions" to ensure the future Business processes are appropriate and "Best-in-class".

- **Discipline to new processes** - Failure at any level to fully comply with new Policies & Procedures and disciplines; with introduce significant risk to the project.

  The Business Process Re-engineering (BPR) for the project will require a major change to the process and discipline requirements of all << COMPANY NAME >> employees.

- **"Big Bang" Implementation** – Implementing all modules for an enterprise at the same time is called "Big Bang", and is considered to be a significant "Risk contributor".

The tight time frame and budget, dictate the "Big Bang" approach. This is caused, not only by the high resource demand, but also starting all the new business processes and systems at the same time.

Development & Implementation Risks

- **Data Migration** – The current data may not be able to be cleaned up, described and migrated in the required timeframe. The project requires the data to be clean, documented and ready to migrate by mid May.

- **Scope Change** – If << COMPANY NAME >> needs more functionality than planned. This may introduce "Scope-creep" to implement extra functionality.

- **Testing** – Failure to provide the necessary resources, inability to get appropriate level expertise, developing the scenarios and implementing automated testing tools within the timeframe will introduce significant risk. The tools are necessary for functionality, volume testing and regression testing.

Vendor Risks

- **Implementation capability** – The vendor is incapable of implementing an enterprise solution. This project depends on the competence of the vendor to implement an enterprise solution; rather than a software installation.

- **Vendor's "Multi Vendor Field Service" expertise** – The Vendor is unable to help << COMPANY NAME >> with the sufficient level of "best practice" and business systems advice, and does not exhibit a thorough understanding of the << COMPANY NAME >>'s type of business.

- **System interfaces** – The vendor is incapable of providing the necessary system interfaces within the time and budget.

- **Vendor Support -** The vendor may not be able to provide the level and timeliness of support. There is evidence that the vendor has a support problem and poor vision on how to fix it in the short term.

Infrastructure Risks

- **IT Hardware support** – The IT group may not have sufficient, appropriately trained, staff to build and support the hardware needs of the project. This would add significant cost and delay to the project.

- **IT Network (WAN/LAN)** - The IT group may not have sufficient capability or incentive to support the network response level of service (LOS) required support the project and ongoing requirements of the new systems.

- **Floor-space** – Without sufficient floor space for dedicated project works the project will be placed at significant risk. The Project team needs sufficient floor space and facilities to conduct lengthy workshops and activities. (Project facilitation room, breakout rooms, workstations, PM office, furniture, etc.)

WHY – SERVICE LEVEL MANAGEMENT

Why

As enterprises become increasingly dependent on IT, they demand a higher quality of service.

By creating an IT Service Management (ITSM) strategy, enterprises are able to maximize end-user productivity, improve operational effectiveness and enhance overall business performance. Additionally, the effort creates a forum for communication between the IS organization and the business units. Also an ITSM strategy provides the basis for integrating IT measurement into operational and strategic IT management. In most cases, however, service management is not well-defined or not defined at all.

Service Level Management principles form the basis on how to contribute to an ITSM culture to ensure that the right services with the appropriate quality are delivered, at the right cost to end users.

Goal

To maintain and improve IT Service quality, through a constant cycle of agreeing, monitoring and reporting upon IT Service achievements and instigation of actions to eradicate poor service - in line with business or Cost justification. Through these methods, a better relationship between IT and its Customers can be developed.

Activities

Identification

- Analyzing current services and Service Level Requirements
- Recording the current service provision in a Service Catalogue.

Definition

Matching & customizing (with the customer) of the right service provision against the right costs:

- Service Catalogue
- Demands of the customer (Service Level Requirements).

Agreement (Defining and signing SLA/s)

- Service Level Agreements, supported by: Operational Level Agreements (OLAs) and Underpinning Contracts

Monitoring

- Measuring the actual service levels against the agreed service levels

Reporting

- Reporting on the service provision (to the customer and the IT organization)

Evaluation (review)

- Evaluate the service provision with the customer
- Match & customize: adjust service provision if required? (SIP, SQP)
- Match & customize: adjust SLA if required?

Results

SLR (Service Level Requirements)

- Detailed recording of the customers' needs
- Blueprint for defining, adapting and revising of services

Service Spec Sheets (Service Specifications)

- Connection between functionality (externally / customer focused) and technicalities (internally / IT organization focused)

Service Catalogue

- Detailed survey of available services
- Detailed survey of available service levels
- Derived from the Service Spec Sheets, but written in "customer terminology"

SLA (Service Level Agreement)

The written agreement between the provider and the customer (business representative)

Service Level Achievements -The Service Levels that are realized

SIP (Service Improvement Programme / Plan)

Actions, phases and delivery dates for improvement of a service

SQP (Service Quality Program / Plan)

- Management information for steering the IT organization
- Process parameters of the Service Management processes and the operational management
- Key Performance Indicators:
  - Incident Management: resolution times for levels of impact
  - Change Management: processing times and costs of routine changes

OLA (Operational Level Agreement) or SPA (Service Provisioning Agreement)

A written agreement with another internal IT department to support the SLA

UC (Underpinning Contract) **a written agreement with an external IT supplier**

Cost

The costs associated with implementing and executing **SLM** include:

- Staff costs (salaries, training, recruitment costs, consultancy - if needed), both initial and ongoing
- Accommodation costs (physical space for staff, documentation space, etc.)
- Support tools (monitoring and reporting, plus some element of integrated **Service Management** tools)
- Hardware on which to run these tools
- Marketing costs e.g. production of **Service Catalogue**

Benefits

- IT **Services** are designed to meet Service Level Requirements and focused on key business areas, with specific targets.

- Improved relationships with satisfied Customers
- Both parties to the agreement have a clearer view of roles and responsibilities
- Management of Expectations
- Service monitoring allows weak areas to be identified, so that remedial action can be taken (if there is a justifiable business case), thus improving future service quality
- Service monitoring also shows where **Customer** or **User** actions are causing the fault and so identify where working efficiency and/or training can be improved
- **SLM** underpins supplier management (and vice versa)
- **SLA** can be used as a basis for **Charging** - and helps demonstrate what value Customers are receiving for their money.

The cumulative effect should lead to a gradual improvement in service quality and an overall reduction in the **Cost** of service provision.

FURTHER INFORMATION

For more information on other products available from The Art of Service, you can visit our website: http://www.theartofservice.com

If you found this guide helpful, you can find more publications from The Art of Service at: http://www.amazon.com

INDEX*